WITHDRAWN

ALSO BY ALISON GRIFFITHS AND DAVID CRUISE

Wild Horse Annie

Vancouver

The Portfolio Doctor

On South Mountain

The Great Adventure

Net Worth

Lords of the Line

Fleecing the Lamb

COUNT ON
YOURSELF

TAKE CHARGE OF YOUR MONEY

ALISON GRIFFITHS

A Touchstone Book
Published by Simon & Schuster
New York   London   Toronto   Sydney   New Delhi

Touchstone
A Division of Simon & Schuster, Inc.
1230 Avenue of the Americas
New York, NY 10020

Copyright © 2012 by Alison Griffiths

All rights reserved, including the right to reproduce this book or portions
thereof in any form whatsoever. For information address Touchstone Subsidiary
Rights Department, 1230 Avenue of the Americas, New York, NY 10020.

This Touchstone export edition January 2012

TOUCHSTONE and colophon are registered trademarks
of Simon & Schuster, Inc.

For information about special discounts for bulk purchases,
please contact Simon & Schuster Special Sales at 1-800-268-3216 or
CustomerService@simonandschuster.ca.

Designed by Akasha Archer

Manufactured in the United States of America

10 9 8 7 6 5 4 3 2 1

ISBN 978-1-4391-8931-3
ISBN 978-1-4391-8935-1 (ebook)

For David

This is book number 11 from team Cruise/Griffiths
and the only one without your name,
but your skills, voice, and incredible editing are everywhere

ACKNOWLEDGEMENTS

I am hugely indebted to hundreds of academics and industry experts who have provided information, research, and opinions not only for this book but throughout my years as a financial journalist and author. I couldn't begin to thank them all, but I hope those of you I have called upon over the last twenty years know that I feel tremendous gratitude.

However, one must be singled out and that is Eric Kirzner. I first started working with Eric, who is a renowned economist and academic, way back in the late 1990s. Eric's ideas are the foundation of the investing section of this book.

I also want to mention Barbara Stewart of Cumberland Private Wealth Management in Toronto. Her insight and information have made me a better financial writer as she has helped me connect the dots between emotion and money. She even got me going to yoga. I am also lucky to have had much input from Dan Hallett, Michael Hill, Michael Chow, and Janet Freedman, particularly in the early days.

I am grateful to my colleagues who cover personal finance and investing for magazines, newspapers, and the cyberworld. I've never asked a question or requested an old article or even asked for advice and been turned down. Those of us who work in this increasingly competitive world know how hard it is to carve your niche, stay in the forefront of the changing financial world, and maintain a public profile at the same time.

In no particular order—Rob Carrick, Jonathan Chevreau, Pat

Foran, Patrick McKeough, Ellen Roseman, David Olive, Madhavi Acharya-Tom Yew, Ken Kivenko, Caroline Cakebread, Gordon Pape, Evelyn Jacks, Larry MacDonald, Bryan Borzykowski, Dan Bortolotti, Norm Rothery, Rudy Luuko, Krystal Yee, and Kelley Keehn, to name just a few; plus the many bloggers I have come to know in recent years who are all playing an important educational and journalistic role in the increasingly complex financial world.

My daughters, Claudia and Quinn, and son-in-law Jeff have been incredibly supportive and never complain when I use them as examples in my columns. I'm a lucky mom and grandmother.

My dear old dad has always been very interested in investing, and his experiences made me pay much more attention to how the industry treats seniors. Also, my sister Fiona is always so willing to lend an ear, attend seminars, and discuss content and case studies.

The production crew of *Maxed Out*, and most especially my amazing producer Anne Francis, taught me a lot about money in the television sphere during the years I hosted the show. It's tough to turn debt into drama but they did it.

And speaking of debt, Laurie Campbell, executive director of Credit Canada, a charity and national leader in debt and credit counseling, and her amazing staff have been an education to me of a different sort. Serving as a director has refined and expanded my financial knowledge.

I've had great readers over the years. Your questions and sometimes criticisms have forced me to stay on top of research and never take a statistic for granted.

Though I am somewhat tough on certain aspects of the financial services industry, the major banks, brokerages, and other firms that exist in the field are always eager to illuminate writers such as myself. Many are now doing excellent work to educate and increase Canadians' financial literacy. Other firms such as Morningstar and Dalbar have unstintingly provided research and data for me.

Kevin Hanson, president of Simon & Schuster Canada, has been my champion for many years, and Alison Clarke has been an insightful sounding board for *Count On Yourself.* I'm sorry the writing has ended, if only for the loss of those wonderful lunches and conversations. Janice Weaver was a wonderful editor and masterful in a subject area new to her.

I am lucky to have actor Barry Flatman in my corner. He is the personification of enthusiasm and great ideas. Just a few words with him always brightens my day. Similarly, Martin Harbury has taught me that sometimes you just gotta do what you gotta do in life and make the best of it. He is a fine producer and so much more. Also Jeanne Beker has provided such encouragement. I feel strong standing in her shadow.

And finally, my old friend and former agent David Colbert helped me through a very tough professional period while writing this book and saved me a big chunk of money in the process.

But in the end, it is one man who makes it all possible—David Cruise—my lifelong partner in every sense of the word. Thank you. Now please pour the wine.

CONTENTS

INTRODUCTION

The financial books that fly off the shelves tend to have zingy titles that include seductive words like *rich, independence, wealth, retire early, millionaire*—things we all yearn for. I struggled unsuccessfully to find my own title for this book until one day I sat down for lunch with my publishers, Kevin Hanson and Alison Clarke. We began talking about how helpless—even stupid—so many of us feel when it comes to money and investing. We are bombarded by financial products and expert opinions and by an army of advisers and fund managers cajoling us to hand over our money—and leave it to those who know what they are doing. To make matters worse, every day seems to bring an economic event in a far-flung country, or even just across the border, threatening to break the nest eggs we have worked so hard to accumulate.

We've also become convinced that we can't take care of (in other words, invest) our hard-earned savings. It is too complex, we're told. There are minefields everywhere. If we take on the task, we risk losing everything. Even financial paragons who file their taxes early, live completely within their means, save regularly, and never miss a bill payment are reluctant to take control of the money they are setting aside for retirement. That's a job for those with lots of initials behind their names, or so the reasoning goes.

But I believe—no, I *know*—that when it comes to *your* money, there's no one better to count on than yourself. If people could develop this confidence, I said to my publishers at lunch that day, they would be stronger financially and, eventually, richer. Kevin and Alison looked at each other, then said in unison, "That's the book title—*Count On Yourself*!"

My goal in *Count On Yourself* is to give you the confidence and tools to set up and monitor a simple, safe, and low-fee investment portfolio. Or if you prefer to use an adviser, the tools and knowledge in this book will allow you to ask the right questions, which in turn will help you keep your fees low and enable you to evaluate the person who is making money from your money.

Most people shy away from investing because they are intimidated by the numbers. Since this is a book about investing, it's impossible to write it without using any numbers at all. But I've kept them to a minimum because, in the end, my style of investing is far less about numbers and far more about who you are as a person. It's about developing a plan you can understand and follow. I've also tried to de-jargonize the world of money. All the bafflegab, acronyms, and complex terms only benefit an industry that profits from our confusion.

The first part of *Count On Yourself* explores our attitudes toward money and the obstacles that stop us from being our own financial boss. Once you kick aside those obstacles—most of which have been set in our path to keep us from managing our own money—you will find that my simple investing program is not only doable but also refreshingly comprehensible.

The second part of *Count On Yourself* takes you through a financial closet cleaning. But don't worry—I won't hector you about debt, chide you for over-consumption, or harangue you about cost-cutting. There are plenty of personal finance books that do just that. Instead, I'll give you some straightforward steps to help you become organized and to get you comfortable with the idea of taking control of your investments. This stage is about simplification and learning how to pay attention financially. Like warm-up exercises before a workout, these organizational steps will prepare your financial muscles to face what scares us most—investing our precious dough.

The third part of *Count On Yourself* shows you how to evaluate your situation and needs, which is a critical element in creating an investment portfolio that works for you. Here you will discover the true essence of smart investing and learn the money-making secrets that the financial services industry doesn't want you to know.

The final part of *Count On Yourself* walks you through a straightforward process (called passive investing) and introduces you to a group of low-fee, low-stress, and understandable sample portfolios. These will outperform most mutual fund portfolios and even provide better returns than many of the complex stock and bond portfolios developed by wealth managers for high-net-worth clients.

When you are finished *Count On Yourself*, you will be able to take control of your investing life with a plan that strips away the confusion and unnecessary complexity so endemic in the financial industry today. Best of all, your low-fee, comprehensible investment portfolio will only require a maximum of thirty minutes a month to maintain. Yes, it will be *that* simple.

Count on yourself for thirty minutes a month. Everyone else is making money from your money, so maybe it is time you turned the tables and made some money for yourself. I know you can do it, and I'm here to help.

PART 1

MONEY: THE FINAL TABOO

CHAPTER 1

Me and Money

I have been thinking about writing *Count On Yourself* for years—twenty of them, to be exact. The rough nugget of an idea has been a rock tumbling in a polisher, with the grit of life smoothing and refining it. The concept has been shaped by my exposure to the financial experiences of thousands of others, my conversations with experts and academics, and my own family's financial triumphs and tragedies. Though at its heart this is a book about investments, it also contains a dash of memoir. I didn't intend this, but when I realized that money is the one thing, besides breath itself, that accompanies everyone from cradle to grave, I knew a book on the subject should have as much to do with living and loving as it did with coins and bills.

Money is central to our lives, and not just because we may feel happier when we have more of it. How we earn, save, spend, and invest defines us and offers a unique window into our personalities. Money is also very personal and intimate, so much so that financial advisers sometimes assume the role of counsellor and therapist.

Occasionally people ask if I get bored writing about money and investments—surely dry subjects, they say. I'm always surprised. Through money, I get to pry into every aspect of the human experience: life, death, birth, inheritance, sex, retirement, and politics. Dull? Not on your life!

Back to those twenty years during which the idea for this book was incubating. If you take any two-decade period in most people's lives, a lot happens. I'm no different. Our children grew up. Our younger daughter, Quinn, went off to study science at university, then took a hard left toward her true passion, cooking. (She is now months away from becoming a chef.) Her older sister, Claudia, met a tall, handsome stranger, Jeff, and produced a delightful son, Jack Gregory. David's father, Jack, died; my mother, Patricia, died; four beloved pooches—Ben, Tip, Blue, and Toby—barked off to doggie heaven after long, happy lives; and two horses—a stillborn quarter horse filly, and Fogerty, a Tennessee walking horse—met their maker far too early. The horses and dogs were joined by a menagerie of rabbits, guinea pigs, rats, cats, and all manner of abandoned or injured critters.

We over-renovated one house, sensibly renovated another, and took a handful of vacations. One was inexpensive and completely perfect—a shabby rented RV ramble through southern California during one of the coldest, rainiest Decembers on record. (It's amazing how much fun you can have crammed into an RV in the middle of the desert with two girls, a bunch of art supplies, and the wind and rain battering the tin can!) Another was expensive and also completely perfect—a trip to the Big Island of Hawaii for ten days of luxuriating in a sprawling thatched cottage. I spent my time on a black sand beach, playing with my kids and overindulging every night.

During the last twenty years, I've worn a lot of different hats—sometimes too many. No question, this writer's life has been full to the bursting. With my long-time life and writing partner, David Cruise, I've written a novel, nine non-fiction books, and a television movie based on a book we wrote in 1991 called *Net Worth: Exploding the Myths of Pro Hockey*. I've been a host on radio and television, including three seasons with *Maxed Out*, a financial makeover show. I once stepped into the shoes of the legendary Peter Gzowski to host CBC Radio's *Morningside*—a dream come true, though nerve-racking at the same time. There have been newspaper and magazine articles, radio and TV stories, and documentaries and columns numbering in the thousands on subjects ranging from fitness and pets to travel and business.

$

The Cruise–Griffiths Clan

The investing and personal finance side of my career took root after a life-changing event in the early 1990s. Our younger daughter contracted meningitis at the age of four in Victoria, BC, where we lived in a marvellous waterfront house that we expected would be the family home for the rest of our lives. The lethal bacteria took hold in the wake of a typical childhood cold. In less than a day, Quinn went from a happy, dancing kid to the brink of death. Meningitis destroyed her auditory nerves, frying them like a wick soaked with gasoline and set on fire. The conflagration was so fierce and the swelling in her brain so severe that in the corridor one night, I overheard her team of doctors debating whether we should be told she was going to die. The head pediatrician convinced them to wait until the morning.

After weeks in intensive care and more weeks in a children's ward, Quinn beat back the disease and emerged into the sunlight having lost nearly half her body weight. She looked like a waif and barely seemed to grow for a year. Along with the auditory nerves, the balance centres in her middle ear were affected. One person helpfully told us of a little boy who'd had meningitis a few years earlier and still hadn't recovered his balance. He ate his meals at the kitchen table tied to his chair with a hockey helmet on his head in case he keeled over.

While Quinn was recovering in hospital, David's eighty-four-year-old father fell ill; he died the week after we brought our daughter home. We were shattered both emotionally and physically by it all. David developed a severe case of sciatica and couldn't sit or stand without pain, Claudia became withdrawn and difficult, and I went days without sleeping. We lost a year of income because we had to delay one nearly finished book and lost the contract on another.

We abandoned our dream to write fiction as it became clear that caring for and educating a child who had suddenly lost all language was going to be nearly a full-time job. But we kept the family together and muddled through this incredibly tough period despite the personal and financial strain.

$

My personal quest to understand money—a quest that led me to write this book—is largely a result of that turn in our lives. I began to realize in the years after meningitis struck that life and money combine to resemble an ocean wave. So often we are carried along like incompetent surfers hoping to stay upright and praying that if we fall we will be washed safely up on shore.

Twice in my life I've been caught in rip currents, or undertows. Though I was a Canadian record–holding swimmer as a teenager, I was terrified both times. Water was my friend in the pool, but I didn't understand this open-water beast that had me in its clutches; in my panic, I did all the wrong things. Money is just like that—it panics us and we make poor decisions.

I've spent much of my life near the ocean, and now, living in southwestern Ontario, the Great Lakes are not far. They often seem benign—they are fresh water after all, not the impenetrable, incomprehensible briny ocean depths—but I have heard of more deaths and accidents on lakes than I can recall in twenty years on the east coast and almost as many on the west. People continually underestimate how mighty landlocked water can be.

If you'll forgive me stretching the analogy just a bit further, there is something we can learn about money from this. Like water, money has many incarnations: debt, income, savings, investments, insurance, bills, and expenses. When we ignore or underestimate the influence money has over us, we make ourselves vulnerable. And when we fail to pay attention to money because it seems either benign or beyond our control, we become further weakened.

With investing—the act of trying to turn one dollar into two— everything I have just written is intensified. Investing is the part of our financial lives we least understand. It's the aspect of money we have the least control over. As a result, it's the thing we are most likely to hand over to someone else. And once we abrogate control of our investing life, we are far less likely to ask the most basic questions about the financial products we buy—the very things that are supposed to support us during our retirement years.

My husband and I followed this same path just after Quinn became deaf. We received a modest inheritance from David's father, and despite having backgrounds in economics, finance, and investigative journalism, we were easily convinced that investing was a job best left to others. And leave it to others we did—three others, in fact, before we finally learned our lesson.

Adviser 1

Our first adviser was a smart guy who told us he believed in a conservative approach to money management. That fit our inclinations. He talked about bonds and safety. Perfect. What we didn't realize was that he wasn't intending to buy bonds, let them mature, and then buy some more—he actively traded bonds.

When it comes to risk taking, bond traders are a 12 on a scale of 1 to 10. Remember Michael Milken, the junk bond king? But we didn't know—or more to the point, didn't ask—what our adviser was doing. The bottom line looked better each month, and that was all we cared about . . . until the bond market tanked.

Adviser 2

We weren't about to make the same mistake with the second adviser, so we carefully quizzed him about his investment philosophy. He assured us it was conservative all the way. One day he suggested purchasing Royal Trustco preferred shares. They sounded good—no stock market gambling here, just steady dividend payments and a stock price that moved within a narrow range. I've always liked Canadian financial institutions—they're safe and secure. Then Royal Trustco did a very un-Canadian thing and went belly up. What we didn't know was that the adviser had put *all* of our available cash, $50,000, into that one stock. We didn't lose everything, but more than $30,000 was gone. At the beginning, we never asked how much he intended to invest because, quite frankly, it never occurred to us that a trained adviser would put so many eggs into one basket.

Adviser 3

Our next adviser was a very smart woman and a vice-president of a major international brokerage firm. She also professed a conservative approach and emphasized her diligence in researching companies. We decided on a stock portfolio of large companies leavened by, on her recommendation, a handful of mutual funds for niche areas such as health care.

The portfolio did moderately well overall, but the investment in the health care sector mutual fund was a real stinker. This time we asked questions. Our adviser told us not to worry because it was a good investment and would "come back." When it didn't, we fell back on our own skills as investigators and checked it out. Turns out it was one of the worst in its category, had been since the day it was born, and still is to this day. Not only that, but the fund paid among the highest sales commissions to advisers and their firms. When we demanded to know why it was in our portfolio, our adviser admitted that it was on the firm's recommended list, which she was required to follow. Small wonder, considering the high commission! We dumped the fund and the adviser.

For me it was three strikes and you're out with advisers. At that point I resolved to count on myself. But I have one advantage over most of you—I can usually convince someone else to pay me to find out things I want to know. So in 1997, David and I approached Ellen Roseman, then the business editor of the *Toronto Star*, and pitched a weekly column about investing. Soon after, we launched another weekly column, the "Portfolio Doctor," in which we used experts to examine and rehabilitate readers' investments.

Writing thousands of columns over the years—while at the same time brushing shoulders with professionals in the field— helped me to evolve an investment philosophy. And through that process, I concluded the following:

1. Most people can and should take charge of their own investments—although they may want to consult an adviser or use one for the actual mechanics.
2. Even a top adviser doesn't care as much about your money as you do.
3. Simple is best when it comes to investing.
4. Much about the world of investing is simply a magic act.

About the latter: the financial services industry is masterful at directing our eyes away while the business of making profits for themselves takes place out of sight. Much of the complexity about investing is *created*. What can be—and should be—relatively simple is turned into something mysterious.

The truth is we can't be in total control of every aspect of our lives. But we cannot afford to cede control of the money we are saving and investing for our futures—the stakes are too high, the consequences too grave.

Now, isn't that annoying? Why should something as ephemeral as money have such power over us? There are so many more important aspects of life: people to love, jobs to do, kids to raise, and hobbies to pursue. Money doesn't seem to belong in the same room. And yet here I am, pushing money through the door and saying, "Deal with it! You ignore it at your peril."

It's time to take back control of your money from the banks, advisers, brokers, wealth managers, and investment firms. It is long past time to stop throwing your money at mutual funds and other investment products you haven't a clue about. And it is certainly time to stop paying a fortune (your fortune) to people who are doing things with your money that you don't understand.

CHAPTER 2

Friends, Sex, Money, and Wealth

Let's face it—some people just get money right. Years ago a woman in her early forties introduced me to her husband, who had made a string of successful investments in wildly disparate businesses, from trucking to vending machines. Being a professional snoop I asked him to share the secret of his success. He hemmed and hawed until finally his wife chimed in. "I don't think there's any great secret," she said. "He's not that smart. He's just got horseshoes up his ass."

Whether it's because of temperament, hard work, some mysterious genetic code, or a relationship with horseshoes, there are those for whom money is as knowable and conquerable as a swimming pool full of water was for me throughout my competitive youth. But for the rest of us, money plays an uncomfortable role in our lives. We spend an inordinate amount of time tortured by both its absence and its presence.

Part of the reason for this is the taint that money carries. You don't have to practise any particular religion to be familiar with the common theme—money, or the pursuit of it, is evil, corrupt, an obstacle to a good life and even a good death. "It is easier for a camel to go through the eye of a needle than for a rich man to enter the kingdom of God," Jesus told his disciples. There is a clear path through God's door, he was saying, and with money you don't get in. In fact, even if you only *covet* money you've got problems. "For the love of money is a root of all kinds of evil."

The fastest-growing religious group in the world is also uncomfortable with money. Though the Islamic faith accepts money as necessary, there are covenants against using cash to beget more cash (i.e., earning or charging interest). "Whosoever reverts [to devouring interest]," says the Quran, "those, they are the inhabitants of the fire, therein dwelling forever."

This discomfort with money is almost universal—Wall Street sharks notwithstanding—and it pervades everything from education to pop culture. It crosses class, race, and language, and afflicts rich and poor as well as friend and foe.

Case Study: A Ladies' Tea Party, 2009

I'm in the Château Laurier hotel in Ottawa. It is the kind of place where money is deeply embedded in every grand room. You can't help but be impressed by how much wealth has swanned through the brass-fitted doors over its century of existence. Old money. Comfortable money. Patient money. No cares, no worries, no woes.

Not so fast.

I walk up the sweeping staircase to the second floor and into an intimate dining room that, while more utilitarian than the public areas of the hotel, still exudes the unmistakable sheen of wealth. I am here at the request of my friend Sarah, who daily dabbles in millions of dollars and is hosting a thank-you lunch for her clients. My role is to lend moral support and keep the conversation rolling. Throughout the room, there are necks encased in pearls and gold, fingers ringed in diamonds, and wrists encircled by platinum. This is a gathering of wealthy women, no question about it.

Despite the fact that the stated goal of the lunch was to talk about money and investments, no one seemed eager to do so. In fact, when the topic came up the women bristled like hedgehogs. Indeed, despite their obvious wealth, several glasses of wine, and the tasty free lunch, no one looked particularly happy. Well, maybe there was an excuse for their unhappiness: the gathering took place just as the financial system imploded and the real estate market worldwide seemed on the verge of collapse.

I did my best to ease things along, talking about my own investments and offering a little historical perspective on recent events, but nothing worked. These women simply did not want to talk about money—not even to complain.

$

Afterwards, Sarah bemoaned the women's reticence to discuss much of anything to do with money. "Not one of them is going to be hurt in the long term by this market meltdown," she said, "but I am getting panicked phone calls from them day and night about their portfolios. Sometimes I feel like just telling them to shut up."

The women might have been expressing their worries to Sarah, but out in public—even in the friendly environment of the Château Laurier hotel with a group of like-minded acquaintances—they kept their thoughts about money generally, and any revelations about their individual situations, tightly shuttered.

As I pondered the ladies at the Château Laurier, I realized they weren't the only ones reticent to talk about money.

$

Case Study: Lori, 49, art gallery owner

Lori is a good friend of twenty years who lives in Vancouver. One night a few years ago, we went out for dinner. As soon as we sat down, she blurted out that she had a vague but persistent pain in her female parts. She'd just completed a battery of medical tests, she said, but didn't have a diagnosis yet. She was terrified that she'd contracted a sexually transmitted disease from a brief liaison on a singles' cruise and had possibly passed it on to her new husband.

As we ate, she spoke, in excruciating detail, of what the doctor did and said. I'm not squeamish, but as the evening wore on I kept thinking that it was a whole lot more than I needed to know. Just as we were tucking into our Grand Marnier soufflés, she began talking about not having had an orgasm in far too long and her fears that, at the age of forty-nine, she might not ever have one again.

Over the years, Lori and I have had many conversations, though none nearly so graphic. In terms of money, we've complained about the high cost of gasoline and worried about our offspring's debt loads and their occasional lack of financial responsibility. And we've confessed to stupid purchases and celebrated fabulous finds. But when it comes to personal finances, all I know about Lori is that she has been a diligent saver her entire life. During our many conversations over the twenty years of our friendship, we've never really talked about what we do with our savings. No, that's not quite right—I have talked about mine, but she's never said a word about hers. I've shared my panic at the financial strain of trying to raise two children, one of them deaf, on a writer's earnings. I've bemoaned our lack of savings in our early years. I've admitted my financial failures. But all I have ever known about Lori's finances is that she saves her money assiduously.

$

Since I became a personal finance journalist, I've given Lori the occasional opening to discuss her investments, especially after the recent financial crisis and resulting recession. I wasn't prying; I was concerned that she was paying excessive fees for poorly performing mutual funds, like so many whose portfolios I'd looked at in the course of writing my column. And I wondered if she was getting good advice from her adviser, who is also a long-time friend of hers. I've seen before how having a friend for an adviser can make it much more difficult to question him or her about your investments. I'm not a licensed adviser and sell no product, so any discussion Lori and I had would reflect only my own beliefs and research. But not a bite; she has always deflected to another topic.

Now, I don't hesitate to ask Lori's advice about gardening, an area in which she has expertise. She's also terrific with colour, and I've borrowed her aesthetic eye and her taste to help me decorate. She knows animals well, and I would seek advice there too. But she has never asked me for the slightest help with, or information about, her investments.

I suspected that Lori, like most Canadians, took a serious beating after the global financial crisis. Through my column, I saw some portfolios with losses of more than 50 per cent. But even in the midst of that cataclysm, she still couldn't bring herself to lift her financial skirts and expose what she had to a close friend.

For a long time, I thought Lori's reticence was just an anomaly. Surely most people don't hesitate to seek counsel from friends who have a specific expertise. But as I thought more about it, I realized that in the nearly twenty years I've been writing about business and finance, I have never had a friend—or even an acquaintance—reveal to me what they have or what they do with it.

About this time I came across a quote that gave me some insight into the issue. "Our finances were private," wrote Nick Cohen, a columnist with the *London Evening Standard* in England.

"Exposing them to others demeaned them and you—the conversational equivalent of stripping off and dancing around naked at a dinner party."

Many people would far rather dance around naked at a dinner party than reveal themselves financially. Another group of other friends drove the truth of this home.

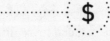

Case Study: The Saddle Bags

I have a group of female friends who I ride with occasionally; we've known each other for years and have shared many stories and not a few secrets. On one gorgeous autumn day, we were cantering over hill and dale, enjoying the multihued leaves and bellowing out our unofficial song—sung to the theme of the old television show *Bonanza*:

> *Get it up!*
> *Get it in!*
> *Get it out!*
> *Don't mess my hair-doooo!*

(There are a variety of other verses to this song, but none are fit for print.)

After a lovely picnic lunch with a bottle of wine, we were on the move again when the conversation wound its way to sex, as it often does with women on horseback. How often, how long, and how? Out of the blue, one of the more reticent riders declared that she and her husband did it every single night, usually in the wee hours. We were all stunned into silence.

Every night?!

We rode along for a bit, each of us processing this information and comparing it to our own sex lives.

Every night?!

Reticent Rider then piped up again. "Of course, it takes less than a minute," she said, "and I go back to sleep right away, so it doesn't bother me."

Less than a minute. Now we all felt a bit better . . . but still.

Back at the barn we opened some beers and coolers and settled ourselves on hay bales to chat while our horses ate their after-trail treats. Another of the women—Sandy, I'll call her—announced that she was taking early retirement. "Maybe," she quipped, "I'll have the time and energy to keep up with her." She cocked her thumb at Reticent Rider.

I used the opportunity to ask Sandy what she was doing with her retirement investments to plan for the transition. She stared at me incredulously and a palpable chill fell upon the group. The question distressed and embarrassed her. She clearly felt it was an intrusion. And she wasn't only embarrassed *by* me—she was embarrassed *for* me. Embarrassed that I would ask her something she wouldn't reveal to anyone except, presumably, her spouse and her adviser. The entire group felt her discomfort, and it took a good twenty minutes for them to get over my faux pas.

$

Just in case you would have reacted the same way the Saddle Bags did, let me remind you that I didn't ask Sandy how much money she had, how well her investments were performing, or even what they were. I was simply curious about her financial plans in the broadest way. Still, it was something she could not or would not share. By the looks on their faces, the other women felt the same way.

I was coming to realize that discomfort in talking about money is very pervasive, but I couldn't quite put my finger on the root cause of it. Discussing sexual practices and bodily functions has been taboo in polite society for at least as long, but the 1960s and 1970s changed our attitudes toward the body. Why hasn't the same openness altered our view of money?

CHAPTER 3

The F-Words

My experiences with friends, colleagues, and readers convinced me that most people are more comfortable talking about sex than money. Money occupies an even more intimate and private place in our hearts and souls. Though both sex and lucre have long been considered somewhat shameful, there is something about money that makes us even more ill at ease, and this is magnified considerably when the specific subject of investing is raised.

When I first broached the concept for *Count On Yourself* to my publisher, there was some concern that readers wouldn't identify with—or, worse, would be turned off by—a book for average folk that included words like *investments* and *portfolios*.

"Portfolio?" scoffed Alison Clarke, director of Sales Operations for Simon & Schuster Canada, when I explained that the book would focus on how to understand and manage a simple investment portfolio. "I don't have a portfolio," she declared.

I asked her if she had an RRSP.

"Oh, yes," she said. "I've got that."

"Then you, Alison Clarke, have a portfolio," I told her. "And here's another bit of news: you also have investments. You are an investor!"

But Alison didn't think of herself that way, and she isn't alone.

At a financial seminar I led for women in film and television, I asked the group of twenty-eight for a show of hands in answer to the following questions:

How many here have a portfolio?   *3 hands*
How many here consider themselves investors?   *12 hands*
How many here have investments?   *18 hands*
How many here have an RRSP?   *26 hands*

I should have seen twenty-six hands for each question. Twenty-six women with twenty-six RRSPs equals twenty-six investors with portfolios.

I began to wonder if trying to convince people that it's possible to create and manage a simple but effective, low-cost investment portfolio was a lost cause. It was becoming clear to me that there's a reason why personal finance books outnumber investment books by at least 30 to 1, and why investing is rarely addressed in general interest books about money.

If your audience isn't even sure they have investments, you have a problem! If your audience is utterly convinced the topic is beyond their comprehension, you have a problem! And if your audience is certain that handling their own investments is as risky as performing brain surgery on themselves, you have a problem!

But there was one group I assumed would feel comfortable talking about money and investing—people who work in the business world, especially those who regularly deal with numbers.

Case Study: Michelle, 39, marketing entrepreneur

Michelle is a high-powered businesswoman whose social media marketing company caught the Facebook/Twitter/foursquare wave early on. I doubt that her five-year-old business grosses less than a million annually—not bad for a woman who was a preschool teacher in her previous life.

Michelle's a self-admitted type A personality who works hard and long, plays hard, and never, ever stops. But when it comes to her investment life, she hits the wall early and often. "It bugs the hell out of me that I don't understand this stuff!" she flares at my very first question about RRSPs. "It irritates me so much I don't want to think about it! In fact, even talking to my adviser gets my blood boiling because I hate, hate, hate not understanding!"

Later, she ruefully admitted, "I know I could understand this stuff—at least I'm pretty sure I *could*—but I don't try. And I don't know why. Once or twice a year I ask my adviser how I am doing. He always tells me I'm doing fine.

"But here's the thing: I *don't* know! I used to think I'll have enough money because I work my butt off and I will always work my butt off. But every now and then I think, 'What happens if . . . ? Then will I have enough money?'"

Michelle is a successful businesswoman, but she clearly didn't feel at all comfortable with her investments. And she was not alone.

I chose my next case study victim—er, subject—because of her obvious facility with numbers and math. I met Mary Ann while serving as a director with Credit Canada, a not-for-profit charitable organization that is a nationwide leader in debt counselling and financial literacy for consumers. She has an MBA with a specialty in statistics and marketing. She impressed me with her smarts and I fully expected her to have absolute control of her financial life, including her investments.

Case Study: Mary Ann, 43, statistical analyst

Mary Ann's job is to measure the effectiveness of marketing campaigns and evaluate the "take-up" by the media of promotional messages. She moves comfortably among statistical paradigms and she easily navigates Gross Rating Points (GRP), Portable People Meters (PPMs), Reach Frequencies, and Outdoor Weight Levels, whatever they are. But when I asked her how she managed her retirement savings (not how much she had!) and the education savings for her two kids, she turtled. Totally.

"Don't talk to me about investing," she sighed. "I just put money in those plans or accounts or whatever."

Whatever? This is a woman who leaves nothing to chance, who understands statistical esoterica. And her response to her investments was to refer to them as "whatever" accounts? This was the complete opposite of what I expected.

"I'm sorry," she said, apologizing for her defensive answer. "It's a legitimate question. I feel like I should be way more on top of that part of my life, and the fact that I'm not makes me feel stupid. And I am not a stupid person. It upsets me, so I delegate. I let my husband do it and I hope to God he gets it right."

At last I was beginning to understand the issue so many of us have with money and investing. It comes down to two F-words—fear and frustration.

I was determined to figure out how best to help readers get control of the investing side of their lives and my publisher suggested a focus group. In late summer 2010, I met with seven women from the book industry who had agreed to talk specifically about their investments. Though all were interested, most had been a bit taken aback—confounded, even—when Alison Clarke told them what the get-together was for. One reacted particularly strongly to the invitation. "She had a look of terror," Alison said with relish. "She made this face like 'Okaaay, but . . .' I really think she was afraid."

The Focus Group

As the discussion got under way, Alison Clarke tried to alleviate the apprehension she'd observed by explaining that the aim was also to give the publishing house and the author—me—some feedback about topic, direction, and title, as well as to generate marketing ideas. This is stuff all book types can sink their teeth and brains into. But first I wanted each person there to tell me a little bit about her personal investing experience.

During the introductions, Sherry, a publishing sales representative, gestured to an empty chair and said, "That's my imaginary friend. I think she does my investments." This earned an appreciative laugh from the group. A little too appreciative, I thought—these women *were* nervous.

Chris was the first person to speak directly about her investments. She launched right into her strategy, describing her adviser as if he were a cross between Mother Teresa and Warren Buffett. She talked knowledgeably about bonds, dividend income, exchange-traded funds, and small cap mutual funds. She even detailed how her adviser gets paid, a feat akin to the average driver weighing in on the subject of torque ratios and tongue weight. If the "average" investor is even aware that her adviser gets paid, she sure as shooting doesn't understand the mechanics of things like trailer fees, management, and load fees—all of which are absent from most mutual fund statements.

As Chris spoke animatedly about her RRSP, her Tax-Free Savings Account (TFSA), and her non-registered, do-it-yourself portfolio, the faces of the other women around the table grew a little stiff.

"Uh-oh," I thought, "this is a real conversation killer. This woman knows what she's doing and is passionate about her investments. No one will want to speak after her."

But just then, Chris paused, and in a softer voice she confided that she became so involved in her own investments because she was afraid of what might happen if she *didn't*. She is one of the legion of workers with no safety net. As the manager of an independent bookstore, she likely has a far lower income than she would have elsewhere in the private sector, and she had no company pension plan.

"Knowing what I'm doing keeps me from worrying I'll end up eating cat food," she asserted. Fear motivated her to learn. It scared her into questioning what her adviser told her, and it made her determined to invest with knowledge and understanding.

Fear paralyzes most people, but it had galvanized Chris. After her confession, the other women took turns admitting their own fears and frustrations about money and investing. Marijke works in a division that publishes business and finance books, and her ex-boyfriend is a successful personal finance author. She ought to have been well informed about and comfortable with money, but she still had the fear and the frustration. "Both my parents were horrific with money," she revealed. "And I've just had a life change. He left, and now it's just me and one income. My fear is about not having any money. But I am paralyzed, in denial. I need to engage with the subject."

It's hard to become engaged when you don't know what you are dealing with, and here's where the financial services industry comes in. We have all been thoroughly and most effectively bamboozled. The separation between our investments and ourselves is now as firmly entrenched as the philosophical separation of church and state.

This is what the financial services industry tells us:

You save your money ▶ We'll invest it ▶ You'll make money

But what often happens is this:

You save your money ▶ We invest it ▶ You pay big fees ▶
We make money ▶ You make money (maybe)

Note that the very last item on the list is "You make money."
Your investments are like a guaranteed income for everyone in
the industry but you. And if you don't have enough money to save
for your retirement, the industry has a solution for that too:

You borrow to make your RRSP contribution (we facilitate it) ▶
The bank makes money ▶ We invest it ▶ You pay big fees ▶
We make money no matter what ▶ You make money
(even bigger maybe)

The weapons in the bamboozle campaign are jargon and
complexity. The more incomprehensible the world of investing
appears to be, the more likely you are to ask someone else to take
care of it for you. The less you understand about your investment
life, the less likely you are to ask questions. Fear of anything usually makes us take a step back.

As parents, we work hard to instil caution in our children.
We don't want them to be afraid of life—just cautious about what
can hurt them. I didn't want my kids growing up afraid to tackle
breakfast in bed on Mother's Day because they were convinced
the stove would turn them into crispy creatures, nor did I want
them flipping pancakes with their bare hands. I would no more
trust another person to teach my children the basics of safety
around my house than I would give a stranger the key to the front
door. Yet, we essentially do that every day when we hand off our
nest eggs to someone else to incubate.

In their hearts, all the women in the focus group except Chris
felt a measure of distress and guilt about handing responsibility for their investments over to someone else. When I gently

questioned them about who was managing their savings and why, I saw on their faces the same looks I used to see when I talked to fellow working moms about daycare. Even those who were thrilled to have their kids in someone else's hands for the day felt guilty about it.

All the women, save Chris, parked their money in financial daycare 24/7. For some, that daycare is a company-sponsored pension plan. An employer pension plan can be lovely to have, but it can also distance you from learning about where your savings are going. Why bother if someone else is taking care of it? You contribute a certain amount each month to a group RRSP and the employer matches it, usually up to 5 or 6 per cent of your salary. But there the connection to your retirement savings ends.

> There are basically three types of workplace pension plans in Canada—defined benefit plans (DB), defined contribution plans (DC), and group RRSPs. With DB plans, the eventual pension is tied to salary and years worked and the payout is guaranteed (though there have been lawsuits about this recently). What you end up with in DC plans and group RRSPs depends on the quality of the underlying investments. There is no guarantee of a specific payment amount upon retirement.

All of the focus group women who had company pensions were contributing to defined contribution plans or group RRSPs. None of them knew what investment products they were buying each month, let alone whether they were good quality. None of them had a clue about how their investment portfolios were performing, or even who was managing their money. And none of them realized that that their return was in no way guaranteed.

One woman joked, "You know how it goes. You get a job, visit HR, and they say, 'Sign here and sign here.' And then every month you put in and the company puts in. Where it goes and what happens to it, I have no idea. I just hope someone is making good decisions with my money."

Hope is the operative word!

Case Study: Ursula Menke, commissioner of the Financial Consumer Agency of Canada

Ursula is a savvy spokeswoman and administrator with more than thirty years of experience in private- and public-sector finance and management. Even so, she got a shock when she examined her defined contribution plan from a previous employer. "The nominal value is the same today as it was thirteen years ago," she said incredulously. "Not only has it not appreciated, but with inflation it has actually depreciated!"

Despite her work experience, Ursula, like the vast majority of employees, had no idea what was in the mix of investments she chose for her retirement plan with that previous employer. And very few employees would inquire about other critical issues, such as fees or the performance and risk level of those investments. "It's asking an awful lot of people who are not comfortable with the whole concept of investing," she acknowledges.

It's scary to consider how much money is in pension plans whose beneficiaries don't have a clue where their money is going or how it is being managed.

Some of the women in the focus group had outside advice of one sort or another for self-directed RRSPs they had opened in addition to their workplace pensions. But those advisers only increased the separation between them and their money. Sheila declared, "I have an adviser, but I haven't talked to him in two years. I have RRSPs, but I don't know how to read the statements. I opened one recently. I looked. I cried. I threw it away."

> Self-directed RRSPs are accounts you open at a brokerage
> firm—often a discount brokerage—and manage yourself
> or with the help of an adviser.

Then this vibrant and intelligent woman went on to flay herself. "I don't know how much my financial adviser makes off me. I'm really interested in investing in stocks, but I don't know how to do it. I'm just completely illiterate in that way."

Janice, this book's editor, chimed in. "I run my own business, create and send invoices, make HST payments, do my own taxes. None of that is an issue. Yet I don't even think investing or managing my savings is something I can do. It seems like a task with no beginning and no end. You think you don't know where to start. And even if you did attempt the job, it would take too much time."

Janice's comment was based on the assumption that a good investment plan takes vast amounts of time to research, analyze, and monitor. This is another belief inculcated by the financial services industry. And it simply isn't true. But the more completely we believe this, the more likely we are to keep paying big fees to have others do the work for us.

Thirty Minutes a Month

I asked the women if they would be interested in a simple investment strategy that would take only thirty minutes a month (or less) to maintain. Yes! they said. If I laid out such a plan for them, would they attempt it? Yes and double yes.

Just for fun, let's try to find those thirty minutes. Think of this next exercise as a gentle warm-up for the task ahead, sort of like financial yoga. Your assignment is to jot down how much time you spend each month on the following:

WHAT	Me	You
MANICURE/PEDICURE	15 minutes	

I have horses, dogs, a barn that needs daily poop-scooping, and a garden. 'Nuff said.

WHAT	Me	You
RECREATIONAL SHOPPING	60 minutes	

I'm not a big mall person, but I do love to browse antique stores and boutiques in cute urban neighbourhoods.

WHAT	Me	You
WATCHING TELEVISION	30 hours (or 1 hour daily)	

Even when I was the host of *Maxed Out*, my husband and I barely watched regular TV, preferring instead to buy a series on DVD and watch an entire season over a month or so.

WHAT	Me	You
STANDING IN LINE FOR COFFEE	0 minutes	

I mostly work at home, so standing in line is a relatively infrequent occurrence for me.

WHAT	Me	You
RECREATIONAL WEB SURFING	35 hours (or 1 hour and 15 minutes daily)	

This one was a little harder to figure, since I often surf for fun during the workday (just like you). Sometimes it's just five or ten minutes looking at horse sites, dog sites, eBay, gardening sites, and whatever else strikes my fancy (or whatever I can think of to avoid work), but it adds up.

WHAT	Me	You
CHECKING FACEBOOK/ MY SPACE/TWITTER/ LINKEDIN	3 hours	

Social media is work to me, so I check in just to check up and then check out again quickly. But Yahoo! tells my husband that Alison Griffiths is in the social room playing poker just about every day. What's that about?

I'm not passing judgment on any of these activities. I certainly do them all throughout the month (except for the standing-in-line-for-coffee thing). Even though I don't watch a lot of TV, I was amazed to realize I devote the equivalent of three-quarters of an entire working week each month to the boob tube. In all, those six activities claim almost seventy hours a month!

I bet most of you will come in around the seventy-hour mark as well. Do any of you still claim not to have enough time to take control of your investments? Yes, you have the time, and you can't afford *not* to use a little bit of it for your investments.

It could be the difference between cat food and caviar in retirement!

When I look at my list, I see how easy it would be to chop off

fifteen minutes a month from surfing the net and watching television. That wouldn't hurt a bit. Now you decide where to find your
thirty minutes. Your financial well-being, not to mention your
mental health, is certainly worth half an hour a month, isn't it?

If you can free up thirty minutes a month (after an initial set-
up process of a couple of days), you can take control of the most
critical part of your financial life—the part that's going to determine if you live well in what is bound to be a long retirement or
semi-retirement. But it isn't going to work if you don't have faith
that you can count on yourself.

PART 2

GET
ORGANIZED

CHAPTER 4

The KISS Principle

After years of reading through RRSPs and other investment portfolios sent by readers of the "Portfolio Doctor" column, and yet more years dissecting indebted train wrecks as host of the television show *Maxed Out*, I uncovered one major impediment to people who were trying to get control of their investments: their financial lives were far too complicated.

When it came to RRSPs and other investment accounts, most of the ones David and I saw while writing our column were almost impossible to decipher and full of holdings with incomprehensible names. Some readers were so desperate for help they sent us multi-page letters detailing the minutiae of their investing experience, even providing their account passwords so we could see for ourselves. Many had run through multiple advisers, and some had four or five different accounts in various institutions. A few tucked cash into the envelopes (which we returned), to compensate for the time it would take us to wade through their portfolios. It didn't matter how much, or how little, money the people had, they were all fearful and frustrated—those F-words again.

There were commonalities among the portfolios we examined: quality holdings were rare; most contained far too many mutual funds; there was excessive risk; no discernible plan was in place; and few investors were making even a modest return. In good times their investments didn't rise as quickly or as high as the stock market, and in bad times their bottom line sank further and more quickly. "Everyone else seems to be making a gazillion dollars," moaned one reader in 2008 as the stock market was peaking, just before the financial crisis hit. "What's wrong with my RRSP?"

While I was contemplating the sad state of readers' portfolios, I read an interview with a rocket scientist that resonated strongly. Jack Crenshaw, an aerospace engineer, was part of the team that put Neil Armstrong and Buzz Aldrin on the moon on July 20, 1969. He plotted Apollo 11's trajectory from Earth to the moon and back using such complex mathematical principles and systems theories that the description of his job reads like a foreign language. Despite the high-level computing, designing, and theorizing, which Crenshaw thrived on, he was mesmerized by simplicity. "I'm a great adherent of the KISS principle," he emphasized. "There's entirely too little of that going around lately."

No one knows who originated the KISS principle, but there's no question it was a powerful catchphrase in the US National Aeronautics and Space Administration (NASA) during the 1960s. Putting a man on the moon was a monumental feat of science and engineering. That something so complex should reference simplicity in the form of KISS is very telling.

The interview with Crenshaw took place in 1999, just months before the collapse of the dot-com fantasy world. What he said that year proved to be equally applicable to money. Indeed, I've become a great adherent of the KISS principle as it applies to money and investments—except I've altered it a bit to "Keep it simple, smarty." It's smart to keep your financial life simple, but there's an entire industry devoted to making it as convoluted as possible. You don't hear mutual fund companies, investment firms, or banks urging us to simplify. On the contrary, they entice us to buy ever more complicated new products that we are told will save us money or make us money. Thus we tend to accumulate all manner of things in our financial closet, and this makes our world increasingly difficult to understand and manage.

If you take away only a few tools and concepts from this book, let KISS be one of them.

Let's have a look at the financial complexity that an average family faces.

Case Study: Aziza, 34, and Marcus, 37

Aziza is a massage therapist and Marcus operates a two-man landscaping/yard maintenance/snowplowing company. They have two children—Janine, eleven, and Peter, nine. From my experience, their list of financial bumpf is pretty near the Canadian norm.

- 2 self-directed RRSPs (his and hers)
- 1 spousal RRSP (Aziza has a higher income and opened it for Marcus)
- 2 moribund RRSPs (from a previous adviser)
- 1 group RRSP (with Aziza's current employer)
- 2 RESPs for their children
- 2 TFSAs
- 5 parental bank accounts
- 2 kids' bank accounts
- 3 bank credit cards
- 4 retail credit cards
- 1 mortgage
- 1 home equity line of credit
- 1 personal line of credit

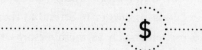

No, your eyes are not deceiving you: twenty-seven bits of financial stuff—pretty normal for a family of four.

Unless you've been living on a desert island or are in training to become a member of a sect that rejects worldly goods, your list is almost certainly lengthy as well. Even if you are single, you may have proportionately more to deal with than those in a relationship. Whatever your life situation, it still amounts to a big load of financial stuff. And we're not finished yet. How many other items are floating around your life? Do you have any of the following?

- Life insurance
- Disability and/or extended care insurance
- Car insurance
- Homeowners' or tenants' insurance
- Student loans
- Car loans or leases
- Buy now, pay later purchases
- Loans from or to a family member
- Internet accounts such as PayPal
- Cellphone plans
- Retail loyalty programs
- Overdraft protection plans
- Extended warranties

More Financial Detritus!

Bear in mind that I'm not talking about actually *paying* for any of the above—I'm just listing the money items that have to be renegotiated or at least examined on a regular basis. These all require you to wrench your mind away from other important things—work, play, lovers, kids—in order to attend to them.

I haven't even added in items such as memberships to clubs (golf, skiing, cycling), timeshares, cottages or RVs, and boats. And this is just what most *ordinary* people have. Things get more complicated if, for instance, you spend time in the United States (for business or pleasure) and need a US dollar credit card and bank account, never mind additional travel and medical insurance.

Everything I've listed requires some kind of care and attention, but the degree varies depending on the item. It may be as simple as renewing a loyalty or membership card or as complex as researching mortgage options at renewal. Some items, like insurance, need attention annually; others, such as a mortgage or a car loan, pop up every few years or so.

Forget the infrequent items, you say. They don't belong on the same list as, say, bank accounts and credit cards. Oh yes, they do! The more infrequently something requires your attention, the more time and brain power you need to refamiliarize yourself with it, the less likely you are to be vigilant, and the more likely you are to gloss over the decision.

When was the last time you actually scrutinized your car, life, or home insurance? After paying little attention to our car insurance for years, I finally took a hard look and discovered that we had a hundred-dollar collision deductible on my twenty-three-year-old Toyota Cressida, which was worth maybe five hundred dollars.

Have you ever compared extended medical/dental plan rates among the various insurers? I have. It takes days and brings on a sudden urge to clean the basement. Anything to get away from the small print, the ifs, ands, or buts, and most especially the numbers.

Having an overcomplicated financial life doesn't just confuse and paralyze—it costs you money because you make rushed, inappropriate, or just plain wrong choices.

Now to the last group of bits and pieces: bills and other expenses. These are the financial obligations that require you to hand over dough on a regular basis. How many of the following do you have?

- Mortgage/rent
- Cable, Internet, television
- Cellphone bills
- Landline bills
- Homeowners' or tenants' insurance

- Car insurance
- Pet insurance
- Credit card bills
- Hydro bills
- Water bills
- Gas bills
- Prescription drugs
- School expenses
- Allowances
- Charitable donations
- Newspaper/magazine/Internet e-zine/other subscriptions
- Alimony/child support
- Daycare/babysitter
- Student loan payments
- Sports dues and fees
- RRSP contributions
- RESP contributions
- TFSA contributions
- Emergency savings contributions
- Bank fees and service charges

"But aren't there overlaps here?" you may be thinking. "Home-owners' insurance, for instance, is on both lists." True, but taking out or renewing house insurance is one brick in the financial load you carry, and paying for it is a second one.

Before I started pruning my personal lists, I had more than eighty bits of financial stuff! Thirty years ago, when David and I first met, he had no credit card and two bank accounts. I had one credit card, two bank accounts, and some Canada Savings Bonds. Granted, it's natural to add complexity as we get older and raise families, but it doesn't need to be the labyrinth that many of us try to negotiate.

The problem with the second list is that you need to give most of these items monthly attention in order to stay on top of them, which sucks up a fair amount of what I like to call your money-minding memory. "Okay, the bills are paid," you say. "I'm done. I'll worry about my mutual funds next month." Our money-minding memory has only so much storage capacity; when bills take up that precious space, it makes it almost impossible to focus on our investments.

"Automatic bill payments!" I hear you shouting. "Set 'em up and forget about 'em." Once again, not so fast. Automatic bill payments are a time saver, and certainly most people pay mortgages, car loans, and often utility bills that way. But the payment is still there—a lighter brick in your financial load but still there. Also, automatic payments need to be monitored because mistakes are sometimes made—and not usually to your advantage.

Finally, if you are part of the sandwich generation, you may still be involved with your children's money, even as you are helping with or exercising control over an older family member's finances.

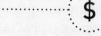

Case Study: Alison Griffiths, 58

I've been slowly taking over my father's finances for several years, with his consent. Today, though I consult with him on everything, I pay his bills, monitor his expenses, invest his savings, and generally keep his financial life running. To my surprise, I've gained a lot of pleasure doing this service for him. However, it does add another layer of complexity to my life. Though he has no debt and a modest RRIF (Registered Retirement Income Fund), there are still quite a few items on my dad's list.

- 3 bank accounts
- 2 GICs
- 1 Canadian ShareOwner Investments account

- 1 non-registered investment account
- 1 RRIF
- 2 credit cards
- 1 life insurance plan
- 1 dental plan
- 6 different pensions (including a wee one from England for fifty dollars a month)
- 1 disability support plan (for which a monthly form must be filled in)
- 1 annual tax return

Twenty more bits of financial stuff!

Now it's your turn to do your own inventory.

Spend five minutes with the list that follows, noting beside each item your own numbers. (Don't forget to include any elderly relatives or other family members, if you have responsibility for their finances.) This is the first step in getting your investment life in order. Consider it a warm-up exercise for your financial muscles. When it's finished, you'll be a lot better organized than you've ever been, and you'll be ready to tackle your investments.

In the next chapter, you are going to see why this exercise is important. You are actually starting to count on yourself, and soon you are going to be able to start taking control of your investment life. I promised that you would eventually be able to manage your own savings and investments in thirty minutes a month, and you will. But that can't happen without a little prep work.

WHAT	HOW MANY
RRSP	
Workplace pension plan	
LIRA—locked-in retirement account	
TFSA	
RESP	
Non-registered investment accounts (personal and joint)	
Chequing accounts (personal and joint)	
Savings accounts (personal and joint)	
Kids' bank accounts	
Bank credit cards	
Personal lines of credit	
Home equity lines of credit	
Car loan/lease	
Student loan/line of credit	
Retail credit cards	
Buy now, pay later purchases	
Life insurance	
Car insurance	
Homeowners'/tenants' insurance	
Kids' insurance (disability, life)	
Pet insurance	
Extended health insurance	
Extended warranties	
Overdraft protection	
Credit card insurance	

Now take another five or ten minutes and write down every single bill you can think of, including anything paid annually.

> A Locked-in Retirement Account (LIRA) holds funds transferred from an employer-sponsored pension or group RRSP. You may make changes in the investments, but you can't withdraw the money until retirement.

Examine your own list. Does it illuminate why you feel a little financially burdened? Is it any surprise that you have neglected some aspects of your financial life? Is it any surprise that when it comes to what I consider the really important areas—nurturing your nest egg and saving for your kids' education—you hand responsibility over to someone else?

You can hardly simplify your life by ignoring the phone bill, but the first step in the Count On Yourself process is to "Keep it simple, smarty" by paring down as much financial junk as you possibly can. How do you do that? Follow, as best you can, Alison's Rule of One:

- 1 chequing account
- 1 savings account
- 1 small line of credit (two or three times the monthly household gross income, for emergency purposes only)
- 1 RESP per family
- 1 TFSA per adult
- 1 RRSP per person
- 1 spousal RRSP (if appropriate)
- 1 non-registered investment account per family (there's an argument to be made for saving and investing outside an RRSP)
- 1 credit card attached to a loyalty program (I recommend these cards if—and only if—you can pay your balance in full each month; otherwise stick to a low-interest, no-frills card)
- 1 low-interest, low-fee backup credit card if you travel a lot

You can violate Alison's Rule of One if you have a very good reason. For example, if you are saving monthly for something special, perhaps a holiday or a wedding, and find it easier or more satisfying to segregate that money, I give you permission to open an extra savings account. I had to open a third account for my father at a bank close to his retirement residence so that he could walk there and withdraw cash. Abiding by the KISS principle, I decided this alternative was less complicated and less work than transferring all his banking and changing all his automatic deposits and withdrawals.

Here's what you don't need:

- Insurance on your credit card balance
- Mortgage insurance (unless your down payment was less than 20 per cent and the insurance is required by your lender)
- Retail credit cards
- Home equity line of credit
- Extended warranties
- An RESP for each child
- Multiple RRSPs
- 3 or more bank credit cards

The next couple of chapters will help you simplify and become far more aware of your financial life. I want you to do this because you can't possibly start to understand your investments or implement the plan I'm going to lay out for you without exposing all your money affairs to the light of day and getting rid of things you don't need. The process is about a state of mind as much as anything else—a clear, in-control state of mind.

CHAPTER 5

Cleaning Your Financial Closet

The goal of cleaning your financial closet is to tidy and organize your affairs so that you're ready and able to tackle your investments. The process will help you prune your financial list and force you to pay attention as you're doing it. Along the way you may uncover some forgotten things—the financial equivalent of an orphaned sock or perhaps your mother's long-lost pearls. Ultimately, cleaning your financial closet aims to accomplish three things:

1. Clarify
2. Simplify
3. Protect

I call the tool you will use to tidy your closet a financial inventory. It exposes clutter while reminding you of things you have either forgotten or simply don't have at your fingertips. Not that many years ago the process would have been quick and straightforward, but it has grown ever more complicated since the Internet became the chief medium of financial transactions. Virtually everything to do with money—from creating a budget to paying bills and playing the stock market—can be accomplished with a computer or a smart phone. What's more, it can be done night or day, in your car, at a coffee shop, or in an airport. The Internet makes our lives simultaneously easier and more complicated because every single financial transaction or account has a cyberguard at the gate in the form of usernames, passwords, PINs, and security questions. If you lose the keys to the kingdom, you'll have a world of trouble getting back in the door. At best it's a frustrating waste of time re-creating or recovering passwords or PINs. At worst it entails futile hours on the phone or—heaven forbid!—an actual visit to the bank to sort things out.

Two events convinced me of the need for a financial inventory that I could get at in the case of emergency. The first happened in 2003, when lightning struck. David and I were sitting in our home office, a lovely, large space that was once the formal living room of our 1849 farmhouse. Four enormous windows looked over the gardens and flooded our desks with natural light.

Just then, I heard a thunderous crack. Something whizzed by my ear, and our older daughter, Claudia, having a bath upstairs, screamed. I thought she'd been shot. I dashed toward the bathroom bellowing her name. She was fine, and had only been startled by the booming noise. When I got back downstairs, David was leaning over in exactly the same position as before, elbows propped on his knees, reading some material for our next book.

"Are you all right?" I squeaked, my voice constricted by fright.

"What's wrong?" he responded placidly.

Our office looked like a tornado had swept through. The outlines of my wireless router and modem were scorched into the desk surface. Smoke rose from the external hard drive. Then I put it together: a lightning bolt had zoomed by my ear. It hit my desk, then ricocheted across the room to fry David's computer—and David.

He hadn't heard or seen anything. He was smiling . . . a little too broadly. I realized shortly that aside from a brief blank-out, David was still David. But our affairs were not. Our computers held all our financial records, which we had backed up on the now also fried external hard drive. We had taken into account the possibility of having one of our computers fail, but not this electronic Armageddon.

Fortunately, a technician was able to rescue most of our data. But we went almost a week without access to any of the keys to our financial kingdom. I was humbled by how little I could remember. Even our password utility didn't help us because it only operated on our home computers. Today you can get a financial aggregator through a commercial site or a financial services provider like a bank. These aggregators act as storage facilities and portals to consolidate multiple accounts from different institutions. But they leave you vulnerable to hacking (remember the Sony and Honda breaches of 2011?), and if you can't get on to the financial aggregator's site, you're dead in the water. My bank's website, for example, has suffered three unexplained outages in the last year.

There are also increasing numbers of "cloud computing" options, from Apple's iCloud and Microsoft Cloud to Google's online document/calendar/spreadsheet programs. All of them allow you to create or upload financial information, or indeed a financial inventory, complete with passwords, etc. These are great but, ultimately, hackable services. And if you can't get on the Internet, you are up the cyber creek with no paddle.

Of course, it isn't just acts of nature that necessitate a financial inventory. My father's experience later in life also underscored the need, albeit for other reasons.

My dear old dad was the absolute monarch of our family's finances. He got his pay from the Royal Canadian Air Force on the last Friday of every month and immediately deposited it in the bank. He kept some cash for himself and placed some more in a plain white envelope, which he sealed and bestowed upon my mother as she mixed their Friday night Manhattans. Mum guarded her housekeeping money zealously. I never knew how much he gave her, and that envelope was a source of endless mystery to me.

In those days, a woman was considered a poor housekeeper and wife if she couldn't make the money last until the end of the month. If she was particularly careful, there would be some left over, and she could use that for herself. My mother was quite brilliant at squirrelling away nickels and dimes for an extra visit to the hairdresser.

Looking back, I think that if all the world's financial affairs had been turned over to women of the "housekeeping money" generation, there would have been no sovereign defaults, no asset-backed commercial paper debacle, no subprime mortgage meltdown. I have this image of a woman like my late mother passing out envelopes to a government minister or a corporate CEO and warning, "When it's gone, it's gone. Don't come back for more."

Back to Dad. Even into his mid-seventies he was well organized, with meticulously maintained files for his bank accounts, investments, and bills. But once online banking and paperless billing entered our lives, his system began to fray. Without all those files to consult, he started losing track.

When Internet security concerns started ramping up in the late-1990s, Dad was no longer able to sign on to his bank accounts with a simple password; he now had usernames, PINs, card numbers, complex passwords, and security questions to remember. Lured in by the ease of virtual investing and banking, he also began opening accounts willy-nilly. Where once there'd been a chequing account, a savings account, and one RRSP, there were suddenly two or three of each at a couple of different banks.

To prompt his fading memory, he wrote notes with clues to himself. When I took over his affairs four years ago, I found scraps of paper with passwords scribbled on them. If a password was associated with a specific account, it was often cryptic. For instance, one investment account had the phrase "favourite movie" scribbled next to it. Unfortunately, Dad couldn't remember what his favourite movie was. Eventually, I found another scrap with *Bridge on the River Kwai* on it. I finally got a hit on KWAI.

I played a guessing game for weeks, trying to uncover my father's online secrets. It really bothered him that he couldn't remember if Poppet, his pet name for my mother, went with his RRIF account or his online stamp club. Burma. Was that a password or the answer to a security question? And those numbers! Birthdays, anniversaries. Which set of digits went with which account?

If ever I was in doubt about the value of a financial inventory, the difficulty I had following my dad's scribbled tracks convinced me that I didn't want to find myself—or put my family—in that predicament years from now.

My first financial inventory started as a basic Excel spreadsheet, and I simply added information as it occurred to me. But by the time the spreadsheet reached five pages I realized I was wasting time hunting through it. Not good, since the whole point of being financially organized and aware is to save time and then use it to make better decisions.

So I divided my original inventory into three, with each new spreadsheet centred on a different category: personal, financial, and investment. These categories are only suggestions, but most of your financial life will fit into them. (When I sat down to write this, I was tempted to come up with a cuddlier alternative to the word *investment*, but you're going to have to get used to it sometime—after all, it's where I'm leading you.)

The Personal Inventory

The personal inventory is the easiest to put in place, and while it may not have much to do with your investment or financial life, it helps you get into the rhythm, a little like decluttering one drawer in your bureau before you tackle the closet.

My guinea pigs for this closet cleaning are Martha and Matt Darcy, who came to me for help in understanding their investments and organizing their financial affairs. I'd used an

Excel spreadsheet to set up my inventory, but Martha was more familiar with the Table function in Word, which also works well and is easy to add to or subtract from, so we used that. You can also download the templates I've set up at www.countonyourself .ca or do it by hand on good old-fashioned paper. The important thing is not *how* you build your inventory but that you actually *do* it. We started with Martha's personal cyber-inventory, and it took us very little time.

Martha Darcy
PERSONAL INVENTORY*

WHAT	USERNAME	LOG IN	PIN	PASSWORD
Vancouver Lily Club	marthadarcy			ilovelily
North American Lily Society	Martha Darcy			ilovelily
eBay		martha&matt		&lily2
Kijiji	mdarcy2008			billycat
New York Times online	mdarcy2008@ yahoo.com			ilovelily
Facebook	mdarcy2008@ yahoo.com			&lily
RealtyTrac (US foreclosure site)	mdarcy2008@ yahoo.com	martha-darcy		sedona
Skype	marthaandmatt			darcyhome
YouTube	marthad2008			ilovelily
lilygal@blogspot .com	Martha Darcy			ilovelily

* Of course, the passwords, PINs and usernames listed here are not real, but they are similar in style to those Martha had created for herself.

WHAT	USERNAME	LOG IN	PIN	PASSWORD
vanpenny pinchers@ twitter.com		Penny Pinchers		savedough
Apple	mdarcy2008			91ndnd41
Aeroplan	111 222 333		121212	4109
Air Miles	marthadarcy			610205
Acme Security Lily Club alarm	112233 (master code)			
SkinOrganix		mdarcy2008		lilies
Primary email	mdarcy2008@ yahoo.com			$lily2
Lily Club email	vanlily@ hotmail.com			coastlily
triclubtraining .com	marthaandmatt			mandm
Secondary email	darcy.martha@ gmail.com			justrun
We Publish		marthabooks		darcyphotos
BusinessCards Direct		Martha Darcy		billycat (Hint: first cat)

Before we started, Martha guessed that her list would be ten to twelve items long, but after fifteen minutes it was up to twenty-three and counting. If yours is even longer, you might want to refine it by adding subcategories such as Hobbies, Family, Home and Garden, Miscellaneous, and so on. Don't stress about it. The idea is to get everything down first.

When Martha and I reviewed her personal inventory, a couple of things stood out. First, she has far too many passwords—fifteen different ones, to be exact. I suggested she prune them down to four or five. Some she couldn't change. Aeroplan, for example, requires numerals rather than letters and Apple requires a combinations of at least eight numerals and letters.

Security experts advise that passwords be six to eight characters long, with at least one symbol, one number, and one capital letter per password. Passwords for personal sites should be different from those for financial sites. If personal sites are hacked your financial security won't be breached.

Next, Martha pointed out that some of the items on the list were obsolete. Years ago, for instance, she and Matt had fantasized about buying a second home in Sedona, so she signed up for RealtyTrac, a website that posts alerts and allows you to search homes for sale, foreclosures, and auctions all over the United States. As time passed, however, priorities changed and their Sedona dream fell by the wayside. But RealtyTrac lived on, dinging her for $59.95 US annually.

Martha also realized that she rarely used her old Yahoo! email account, so she sent redirect messages to her contacts. Similarly, she no longer purchased the Skin Organix line of cosmetics she liked because the currency charges on her credit card and shipping costs across the border made it too expensive. But she hadn't cancelled her account and was still paying the $19.99 annual membership fee. On the other hand, though Martha hadn't added a single line to her blog in two years, she elected to keep it, just in case. She had forgotten how to sign on, however, so it took a bit of brain-racking to suss that out. She also retained the Vancouver Penny Pincher Twitter project because, as a sales rep, she found it a pleasurable distraction while waiting for customers.

A couple of months earlier, when I first spoke to Martha about creating a financial inventory and cleaning her financial closet, her eyes had glazed over after a few minutes of conversation. But by the time we hit the twenty-five-minute mark on her personal inventory, she was completely engaged. Martha now realized that she'd been feeling overwhelmed but had no idea how to get control of this aspect of her life. Now she was raring to get on with her financial inventory.

The Financial Inventory

Your financial inventory is the place to list anything having to do with money—bank accounts, RRSPs, investment accounts, your Revenue Canada login, and so on. There are many ways to get started. With my first, I added things as I thought of them, just as we did with Martha's personal inventory. But I soon found it much better to group items into three categories: Bills, Banking, and Miscellaneous. One quick tip, as you go through this exercise, is to keep on hand a couple of months' worth of bank statements, particularly for the account you use to pay most or all of your bills.

In this inventory, there are going to be more variations in passwords, PINs, and usernames. Often, you need different passwords and PIN numbers to access online banking and telephone banking, and you may even need multiple passwords. For instance, I need one password to sign on to my RRSP and non-registered investment accounts, and another to do any buying and selling of investments. But since it's the same company and the same website, I simply use one password for both, which cuts down on the clutter. KISS!

Martha, brimming with confidence, elected to refine her PINs, passwords, and usernames on the go. Also, she decided to err on the side of safety by abbreviating passwords and security questions just in case a cyberthief came calling. I agreed but urged her to make a complete list with full passwords and stash it in a safety deposit box. You can also use one of the burgeoning password- or account-access services (financial aggregators) I mentioned earlier. I'm not in love with this idea, but if you do go this route make sure you also have a hard-copy master list in a safe place.

We never imagine that a family member or friend will have to step in and take over our financial affairs, especially when we are young, but it does happen. In 2010 I had surgery to repair a ruptured eardrum. Afterwards, the hospital bestowed upon me a staph infection, which eventually required a super antibiotic to kill. For a month, my husband had to run every aspect of our lives, from caring for cats, dogs, and horses to overseeing our writing careers, columns, and financial affairs. Thanks to my inventories, he had all the information he needed to take charge of accounts he rarely examines, while I drifted along in a Percocet fog.

Martha elected to pool her financial information with her husband's. Some couples aren't comfortable giving each other access to accounts and security information. Complete financial disclosure is just a bit too intimate. But Martha and Matt had no problem sharing, since they've always deposited their paycheques in a single account and used it to pay the bills.

As for intimate . . .

"Once you've been pit crew for a woman doing a Half Ironman triathlon and contended with vomit (pre-race), diarrhoea (during the race), and severe chafing *down there* (post-race), intimate takes on a whole new meaning," noted Matt wryly.

Nonetheless, going through this closet-cleaning process did unearth a ghost from the past. Cue the spooky music.

Martha and Matt Darcy
FINANCIAL INVENTORY

WHAT	USERNAME	LOG IN	PIN	PASSWORD
Bills, etc.				
Cellular Connect	mdarcy		7304	d——e
Bell land line	mdarcy	darcy.martha@ gmail.com		d——e
U Do It Tax Online		darcy.martha@ gmail.com		d——e

WHAT	USERNAME	LOG IN	PIN	PASSWORD
Hydro online		marthadarcy		d——e
Canada Revenue Agency epass		97863 (access code) Security Hint: fave colour		$—2
Municipal taxes online	Martha Darcy	32 Bedford Rd.	7304	d——e
FedEx online	Martha Darcy	56890 (account number)		
PayPal		darcy.martha@ gmail.com	730481	$—2

Banking/ Credit Cards	Username & Limit	Log In/Card Number	Username & PIN	Password
ABC Virtual Bank 1 high-interest savings account 2 RRSPs		5508 493 2766 (Martha's card) 5508 493 2981 (Matt's card)		i—(Martha) Hint: Martha's first tri run—(Matt) Hint: Fave destination
Big Five Bank 1 chequing account 2 savings accounts 2 credit cards		476 9055 1336 5367 (online banking/credit cards/home equity line of credit)		d——e
Big Five Bank 2 debit cards			7304 (Martha) 0481 (Matt)	Hint: Martha's first tri Hint: Matt's graduation
Big Five Bank Martha's personal line of credit	???	???		???
Down Home Trust	marthaand matt	3223 3123 789 (savings account)		Hint: Where we met

WHAT	USERNAME	LOG IN	PIN	PASSWORD
VISA 2 credit cards	???	4555 6789 4356 (Martha) 4555 1234 5678 (Matt)	7304 (Martha) 481 (Matt)	
MasterCard 1 joint card	???	5444 4321 9876		
Home Depot	???	54 6578 9003 56	???	
Sears	???	6543 4567 0909	???	
Insurance	**Policy Number**	**Beneficiary**	**Amount**	**Password**
All Life Insurance	6549985-MD90	Matt	$200,000 (expires 2030)	Hint: Martha's mother's maiden name
Life insurance (Matt's work policy)	ID#rjr4235	Martha	$100,000	ID number
University of South Carolina (Martha)	???	Andrew Pyle Jr.	$10,000	???

"Who the hell is Andrew Pyle Jr.?" demanded Matt. "And what's he done to deserve ten grand?"

"Ah, Andy."

"So it's Andy now!"

"It was before your time. I just forgot."

"I can't believe you hooked up with someone who called himself Junior!"

"Hey, it was the South! Everyone there is Junior or Bubba."

As it turned out, Martha had taken out an insurance policy after graduating from the University of South Carolina, where she studied on a partial track scholarship. It was a special deal for graduates, and she prepaid to get the best rate. She and Junior had been platonic roommates before they added "benefits" to their friendship. They stayed together through Martha's intern year as a high school guidance counsellor and then started talking about the future. But Junior could no more think of leaving South Carolina for the cold, hard north than Martha could imagine one more muggy southern summer.

She had completely forgotten about the insurance and no longer had any idea what kind of policy it was. When I'd told them to pull out all files relating to financial matters, she'd disinterred an old empty one marked "USC—Insurance" and found Andrew's name jotted down with "$10,000" written on the cover. After some sleuthing, Martha found out that the term policy had expired and there was no retained value.

Before we began working on the financial inventory, I'd asked Martha and Matt to estimate how many entries there would be. Martha was now wised up.

"Twenty-three," she said, doing a quick mental calculation.

"Seventeen," offered Matt.

So far, they were at thirty-two entries. They'd both initially forgotten to include their various life insurance policies among the bills because they pay the premiums annually. They also pay annually for a satellite car-theft protection service and had left that off the list. And they forgot to include their car payments, which come out of their joint credit card monthly to give them the loyalty points. Automatic bill payments are a convenience, but they're easy to overlook.

The other thing we all noticed as we assembled Martha and Matt's financial inventory (which took thirty-seven minutes, by the way) was how much superfluous stuff they had.

An extreme violation of KISS!

Time to do some purging. I recommended they rid themselves of the following. Note, though, that these recommendations may not fit every situation, so don't follow them slavishly. Instead, make your own inventory and consider how best to simplify it. Some women—and indeed, some men—feel uncomfortable sharing all their accounts and credit cards with their partner. If that's you, then have a joint card for most expenses (possibly one linked to a loyalty program) and one separate personal card each.

- Both personal Visa cards (and the other had an annual fee of ninety dollars)
- Both retail credit cards (one was charging 29 per cent interest)
- Down Home Trust savings account (transferred to ABC Virtual)
- Martha's personal line of credit
- Big Five Bank savings accounts (they had small balances but were paying fees on both and already had a better deal with their virtual bank)

There is a hilarious scene in one of my favourite movies, *L.A. Story*, where the hyperactive and child-like Sarah Jessica Parker drags Steve Martin off to Venice Beach to experience the delights of a high colonic. Martin exits on wobbly legs. But Parker is positively purring. Martha and Matt didn't quite need that kind of invasion to achieve a cleansing feeling. They were thrilled to get their financial life down on paper, and they felt far more in control because they were aware. And that awareness gave them the confidence to get rid of stuff they didn't need.

They saved some money by closing accounts, and they took a hard look at their credit cards and credit lines. Their six cards had a total of $80,000 of credit available, and Martha's personal line of credit added a further $55,000. That's a lot of credit; it costs money in fees, and it was having a negative impact on their credit scores.

Improving their credit score was important because Martha

and Matt had a big move planned: they intended to sell their home in the suburbs and move into the city. Being closer to work would save them more than $350 monthly in commuter costs, though it would cost them about $150,000 more on their mortgage. An improved credit score should help them negotiate the best possible rate.

Now that the financial inventory was finished, we were ready to tackle the next challenge—"the bogeyman under the bed," as one of the women in the focus group put it—investments, or more specifically, the investment inventory.

CHAPTER 6

Your Investment Inventory

Even though Martha and Matt had mastered their personal and financial inventories, I could see they were nervous about moving on to their investments. Normally gregarious and expansive, Martha and Matt were quiet and tense. "Easy, easy," I soothed, as if the Darcys were one of my horses spooked by a strange object. "This isn't going to be any more difficult than the previous steps, and it will be even more illuminating—I promise." I resisted the temptation to reach out and scratch them behind the ears.

My strategy for easing Martha and Matt into their investment inventory was actually all equine. When a horse shies, most riders urge it forward to show the animal that what it fears is merely a rock, a mailbox, a bag tossed on the ground. Sometimes this works, but often a struggle ensues. Legs, spurs, reins, voice—all come together to encourage the animal to face its fears.

"You can do it. You're okay. Nothing to be afraid of here. Just a silly rock!" you coax. But the horse isn't listening to you; he's listening to his fears, and those fears are stating unequivocally, "That sure as hell ain't no rock. It's a horse-eating monster."

Many of us have the same "spooked horse" mentality when it comes to investing. We freeze or flee—and sometimes both. We procrastinate, prevaricate, promise—but rarely proceed. Or we turn and run after dumping our investments in someone else's lap (an adviser, spouse, relative). Often, unhappy investors go from adviser to adviser. (I knew one couple who had five different advisers in play at the same time, none of whom knew the others existed.)

"If I don't look at my RRSP statement," we whisper to ourselves, "I won't know how much money I've lost, or I won't feel stupid, confused, and frightened." Or, "I won't have to strain my brain." And, "There! I didn't look, and I didn't feel any of the things I don't want to feel. Perfect! Next month I won't do the same thing again."

Even though fear provokes more complicated responses in humans, the solution to it is much the same as it is with horses: we must find our comfort zone. Martha and Matt thought the point of the personal and financial inventories was simply to get organized, learn to pay attention to what they had, and then simplify to make it easier and cheaper to manage. All true. But I was also working to expand their comfort zones so they'd feel as confident dealing with their investments as they did their bank accounts.

When it comes to investing, we often create this comfort zone by using another individual as a buffer. That person can be a bank manager, an investment adviser, a mortgage broker, or a mutual fund or insurance salesperson. We hide behind the apron strings of "experts," who presumably have the background to tell us what choices to make and when to make them. The problem is that the people standing between you and your money quickly starts to loom very large. Soon, you can't see over, under, or around them, and whatever is going on with your money becomes obscured by their presence.

Today, the financial services industry is mostly about pushing product. And in a world of sell, sell, sell, the idea of doing what's right for an individual investor often gets lost in quotas, marketing objectives, and corporate bottom lines. The goal of this book is to put you in the position of knowing what's right for you. Remember—no one else cares about your money as much as you do!

But before you can take that big step around the person or firm separating you from your money—even if it is just a voice on the phone or figures on a statement—you have to find a level of comfort with your investments. And that is where an investment inventory comes in.

Martha and Matt were now making backing-out noises. They both muttered some variation of the expression "If it ain't broke, don't fix it."

"How do you know it ain't broke?" I asked.

Worry creased their faces. "Oops!" I thought. I'd only meant to nudge them gently, not upset them. This was supposed to be an empowering exercise. There's enough investment fear and frustration out there already.

"Let's make a list of your RRSPs," I said cheerily, sending them off to get their paperwork.

They returned with an assortment of files. I praised them for keeping everything more or less together and for more or less filing their statements and other communication from the banks and Matt's company. The key phrase was "more or less." They'd told me previously that they had three RRSPs and no other investment accounts, but when we dug into the files, the total grew to eight—three for Matt, five for Martha.

Martha and Matt Darcy
INVESTMENT INVENTORY

WHAT	USERNAME	LOG IN	PIN	PASSWORD
Group RRSP (Matt's work)	rjr4235			rjr4235
Big Five Bank RRSP (Martha)		650095		Q5678 (sign on) 5678 (trading)
Big Five Bank RRSP (Matt)		650987		T9012 (sign on) 8761 (trading)

WHAT	USERNAME	LOG IN	PIN	PASSWORD
ABC Virtual Bank RRSP (Martha)		5508 493 2766		ilove——Hint: Martha's first tri
ABC Virtual Bank RRSP (Matt)		5508 493 2981		run——Hint: Fave destination
Hospital pension (from Martha's previous job)	???	???	???	???
Trust Us Wealth Experts RRSP (Martha)	marthasutter	???	???	???
General LifeCoFinancial Group RRSP (Martha)	???	???	???	???
Walt Disney and Ford shares (Matt)	???	???	???	???

Once again, there were surprises. Shortly after graduating, Martha worked for three years in the human resources department of a large hospital services company. It was one of those middle-management jobs where fifty hours a week was the norm and more than fifty-five common—too much for Martha, who wanted a life outside of work, especially to pursue her goal of competing in an Ironman.

When she quit, Martha elected to leave her pension where it was instead of transferring it to a LIRA, cashing it in, or transferring it to an adviser. That was the recommendation of the HR manager, and in my opinion, it was a good one. The pension had a reputation of being well run and generating decent, if not sparkling, returns. I've seen many disasters when employees were encouraged by advisers to commute or transfer a pension and sell the investments in favour of a new portfolio of stocks or mutual funds. Invariably they ended up with poorer returns and far higher management costs.

"This is excellent news," I said. "You've found some money

you'd forgotten about. Don't worry about how much it is right now. Just be happy you've got it."

"You're like a investment philanderer," Matt joked, noting Martha's five accounts.

"Hey! I opened one with Trust Us just after I graduated. That's thinking ahead, isn't it?"

But Martha had also lost track of that account, and because she'd changed addresses numerous times, she no longer received statements. After some digging around, however, she found a receipt for the original deposit.

Martha's investment forgetfulness is far from unique. Many of us have investments trailing behind in one form or another, especially after changing jobs. I've come across people who didn't even realize they had contributed to a workplace pension, much less how much or what it was.

"How much?" Matt demanded.

"Dunno," Martha sighed. "It says here I opened the account with $2,000. That should be worth a ton now, don't you think?" She looked at me expectantly.

"Haven't a clue," I said with a shrug. "RRSPs are just a box. You put cash in them and then use the cash to purchase investments. Until you do that, it's just an empty box." I paused for a moment. "So what investments did you put in the RRSP?" I asked mildly.

I suspected that when Martha opened the account years ago, she was given a choice of investment packages, ranging from low to higher risk. There was likely no discussion about what those packages of investments were, let alone the fees charged or returns over time. She probably chose a medium-risk package, as many people do. Martha never knew specifically what went into the box, only that it was probably mutual funds.

"I don't know." She looked at me blankly. "Is it important?"

"Look at it this way," I said, searching for an analogy. "You know bicycles because you do triathlons. Would you buy a box marked 'Bicycle' without knowing what was inside?"

"Of course not. That would be ridiculous," she snorted. "I

could end up with a mountain bike or a hybrid when I wanted a road bike."

"Exactly. But that's precisely what you did when you plunked down $2,000 for those products marked 'RRSP.' You had no idea what was inside the box."

I was feeling a little guilty about pushing Martha, but I sensed she was at the tipping point. She needed to want to know what was inside the box.

"And would you buy a bicycle without knowing the cost?" I pressed.

"Now that would be really dumb."

"Do you know how much whatever is in that Trust Us RRSP box is costing you every year in terms of fees?"

Martha confessed that she didn't realize there was any cost to investments in her RRSP.

"So you bought something, but you don't know what you bought or how much it cost you," I concluded.

Martha thought for a moment. "When you put it that way, it does sound awfully stupid."

Like most people, she'd never thought of her investments as a purchase like any other, and it had never occurred to her that the investment would cost her for as long as she owned it.

Matt was looking a little smug, but he also had some 'splainin' to do. He'd started out intending to be in charge of the investments in both his and Martha's RRSPs. The adviser at the bank where they'd opened their RRSPs was a nice man and very interested in their lives and goals. Matt dutifully read all the paperwork, filled out the Know Your Client forms, and participated in a Risk Tolerance evaluation. The adviser showed Matt lists of recommended mutual funds, as well as a number of packaged mutual fund portfolios. Matt chose a prepackaged portfolio designed for growth and moderate risk tolerance for their RRSP accounts.

Life got busy, and Matt ended up consulting with the adviser only a handful of times in the ensuing six years. The adviser had called last year to encourage them to open Tax-Free Savings

Accounts (TFSAs) and suggested some investment products they could buy with the funds they deposited.

Matt now had little recollection of their RRSPs beyond the fact that he and Martha were making monthly contributions. "I thought I had a handle on everything, but when the statements arrived, I found I didn't really understand them. We were depositing money through an automatic debit from our chequing account into our two RRSP accounts, so it wasn't like I had any decisions to make."

Matt had a neat stack of statements detailing the brokerage mutual fund holdings in their RRSPs. When I got him to read one, he was surprised he didn't recognize some of the fund names. That was because some of his original ones had merged with other funds, and in a couple of cases the original fund company had been taken over by another one. I counted six such changes in their two accounts.

Martha did a *mea culpa*. "We both should have paid more attention."

"You're paying attention now, and that's what is important," I said encouragingly.

Like Martha, Matt also rediscovered a piece of his financial past when his mother reminded him that his maternal grandfather had given him ten shares of Walt Disney Company and ten shares of Ford Motor Co. on his tenth birthday. Matt loved Disneyland and had visited it with his parents and other family members almost every year until he graduated from high school. He was also a car-crazy kid and built models from hobby kits. His favourites were all Fords. Twenty-nine years later, he had no idea where the shares were or how much they were worth.

I suspected that the stock had been purchased and registered in Matt's name, in trust. Every publicly listed company employs a transfer agent, usually a bank or a trust company, to act as an administrative middleman and maintain records of things like account balances and transactions. The investor relations' departments of Ford and

Disney would put Matt in touch with their respective transfer agents, which would then help him reconnect with his stock.

In the meantime, we did a quick bit of Internet research and a rough calculation. Disney went through some hard times during the recessions of the mid-1990s and over-expansion after that, but those ten Disney shares, purchased for a little more than $500 in 1982, were now worth over $19,000. Add in the dividends and the total was nearly $21,000.

Ford's story was a little bit different. Share prices for the Big Three car manufacturers hit bottom in 2008, but Matt still had made enough for a vacation or to pay for nicer accommodations in Hawaii if Martha ever fulfilled her dream of doing the Kona Coast Ironman Triathlon. What had cost his grandfather a mere $170 for ten-year-old Matt's birthday was now worth $3,300, including dividends.

Part of the allure in buying stocks is the hope of hitting it big. Though Matt had done well with his Disney shares, the financial crisis took an axe to the value of Ford. Stock picking is like that. It is extremely difficult to pick well and consistently over time. That's why investors are funnelled into mutual funds. But as we'll learn later, mutual fund managers face the same challenges as anyone else buying stock in companies—and often they don't surmount them.

Martha and Matt now felt a bit more knowledgeable, and thanks to Disney, Ford, and Martha's forgotten RRSPs, they felt richer as well. I told them they'd earned a dinner out and a good bottle of wine to celebrate.

Before you move on to your own investment inventory, let's review what we've accomplished so far:

1. Personal Inventory: You've created a master list of your personal cyberstuff.
   a. In the process you have, hopefully, pruned away some detritus and saved some money by getting rid of unwanted subscriptions or memberships.

   b. You should also have refined your access to cyberville so you don't have as many passwords, logins, and user-names.

2. Financial Inventory: You've created a master list of your online financial affairs, noting down anything that requires any combination of logins, PINs, and passwords.

   a. You have reduced bank accounts if they number more than two per individual or three to four per couple. (Special circumstances may entail more accounts.)

   b. You have reduced your credit cards to no more than two per person or three per couple (and improved your credit score at the same time).

   c. You have consolidated loans, if possible at lower rates, and reduced limits on home equity and personal lines of credit (and improved your credit score at the same time).

3. Investment Inventory: You have listed all your investment accounts, from RRSPs and company pensions to RESPs, TFSAs, and any non-registered investments (Disney anyone?).

Getting to this point in your investment closet-cleaning exercise is pretty straightforward. But what you really want to know is whether you are on the right investment path, and if your investments are good, fair, or barking bad. Martha and Matt, like many people, didn't have even a basic understanding of what they were buying or what sales and management fees those products carried. This is where it gets more difficult. If an adviser encourages you to buy certain products, he or she is hardly going to recommend you comparison shop for better ones.

I did an analysis of Martha and Matt's holdings in the RRSP accounts at their bank brokerage firm. As expected, I found a welter of mutual funds, a lot of duplication, higher than necessary fees, and uniformly mediocre overall performance. Less than a third of their funds were doing as well as their comparable benchmark stock and bond market indices. (I'll talk about these benchmarks in a later chapter.) Some of their funds were inappropriate for them, and one, a money market fund, was earning them absolutely nothing annually. This was pretty typical of 90 per cent of the portfolios I see on a daily basis—lots of expensive junk.*

After going through this Count On Yourself exercise, Matt and Martha were determined to be in better control of their investments and follow my low-fee, low-maintenance program. At this point, I told them they had three choices:

1. Sell everything and begin again.
2. Sell the funds over time to avoid sales charges.
3. Keep the funds for the time being and start a new account in order to follow the Count On Yourself program.

For Martha and Matt—and anyone else in their situation—the big advantage of selling it all is that it would give them the cash to build a better portfolio at a lower cost. The disadvantage is fees. Many mutual funds are sold with deferred sales charge (DSC), fees that are deducted from the proceeds when you sell them. A given fund may, for example, have a DSC of 6 per cent the first year, 5 per cent the second year, and so on, until the fee declines to zero. If you are buying mutual funds monthly, each new purchase will come with a new schedule of deferred sales charges. If, however, you have no-load funds, such as bank mutual funds, there will be no charge when you sell. (Most fund families allow the sale of 10 per cent of a fund annually with no DSC applied.)

Selling over time to avoid charges is certainly an option, but if you have poor-quality funds with high fees you are probably better off cutting your losses and starting fresh.

---

* Even if you decide not to follow my low-fee, low-maintenance investment plan, I highly recommend you conduct your own Investment Inventory. If nothing else, it will bring clarity to your portfolio and provide an important point of reference. If you feel daunted by the prospect of evaluating your current holdings, you should consider consulting a fee-only or fee-for-service financial adviser. Because these advisers have no product to sell, they can give you unbiased advice. During the initial appointment, which is usually free, the adviser will estimate how much his analysis will cost.

Keeping the funds can work if you have good ones. Do you know? Most people don't. Even if you have the skills to evaluate your holdings, the practice in the mutual fund industry of collapsing poorly performing funds into better ones can disguise subpar performance. There are some excellent mutual funds available; the problem is that most people have no idea how to find them. And if those funds pay lower fees to advisers, there is a good chance they won't recommend them to their clients.

The other disadvantage with this approach is that you will now be dealing with two portfolios, one to hold the mutual funds and one to start the Count On Yourself program. That's a recipe for confusion. Remember, KISS!

One Month Later

Martha and Matt elected to start from scratch and build simpler, lower-fee, and more comprehensible portfolios. They sold all their mutual funds. That did make them a bit nervous, but they were eager to put themselves in the driver's seat and stop paying high fees for investment products that underperformed the broader markets. It took a month to transfer the various accounts and Matt's stock. Here's how it all looked in the end:

WHAT	VALUE	USERNAME	LOG IN	PASSWORD
Group RRSP (Matt's work)	$22,000	mattdarcy@ graffixinc.ca		use ID #rjr4235
Big Five Bank RRSP (Martha)	$48,500		650095	Q5678 (sign-on)
Big Five Bank RRSP (Matt)	$40,000		650987	T9012 (sign-on) 9012 (trading)

WHAT	VALUE	USERNAME	LOG IN	PASSWORD
Big Five Bank (Matt's non-registered account with the Ford and Disney shares)	$24,300		71984	BC7099 (sign-on) 7099 (trading)
Locked-in RRSP (Martha's previous work)	$ 8,900		martha-darcy	HP355-71

Much, much clearer, and oh so comprehensible.

"Happy?" I asked.

"Very!" they chorused.

They hadn't admitted to themselves, or to each other, how much in the dark they'd really been about their investments and retirement savings. We decided that Martha's hospital pension plan contributions would remain there until retirement, and Matt would educate himself about his group RRSP once we had their new investing plan in place.

"Notice anything now that it's all in one place?" I asked.

"We both found some money we'd forgotten about, but we actually thought we had a lot more retirement savings," said Matt.

Matt was thirty-nine and Martha forty-one; they both hoped to be working only part-time by age fifty-five, and they wanted to retire completely by sixty, so a little savings and investment giddy-up was certainly in order.

In the next chapter, we'll take the first step toward putting together your own investment portfolio.

PART 3

MAKE A PLAN

CHAPTER 7

Who Are You?

Putting together a low-fee portfolio that is easy to understand and manage starts with figuring out who you are as an investor. This is a critical question to answer, and you court disaster by neglecting it.

Determining your investment profile is about matching your needs with the options available. We do that all the time, both formally and informally—when we travel, purchase an appliance, buy clothes, or go out for a meal. Often, it's an automatic process. If you have a sensitive stomach, you winnow out spicy restaurants. If you have a small apartment, you don't bother looking at giant washing machines. We can—and should—do the same thing when it comes to investing.

My husband and I took this kind of systematic approach when we bought our first car. We put together a "Who are we?" list, though we called it "Priorities." Here's what we thought was important:

1. Spending limit of $10,000. (We bought new because no one would lend us the money back then for a used car.)
2. Room for two car seats. (One child in hand, another on the way.)
3. Room for one (often dirty) border collie.
4. Manual transmission. (Easier on gas and more fun to drive.)
5. Reliable.

6. Good repair record.
7. Good gas mileage.
8. Good resale value.
9. Red or blue in colour.

Once we had our list and understood our priorities, we read the books, consulted the magazines, and test drove everything in the price range. A Toyota Tercel wagon best fit the bill. (We actually liked the comparable Honda better, because it was sportier, but it cost a thousand dollars more.) With a Tercel shortage sweeping the nation, however, the only colour available was a dreary shade of tan. In the end we met eight of our nine priorities, and since colour was our least important criterion, we decided to live with the bilious beige.

The sad fact is that most of us spend far more time investigating car purchases than we do checking into our investments (or financial advisers). Our priorities list for the car purchase was quick to assemble and then we spent a couple of weeks test driving. You can follow the same process with your investments. And truthfully, can you afford not to? Cars are important to our lives, but there is a lot more at stake with our investments!

After my experience with a series of advisory firms that didn't end up meeting my needs as an investor, I decided it was time to determine who I was and then pick an investment strategy to suit. I realized that I wanted to know exactly what I owned, and that I really disliked being unable to understand how well my investments were performing without an advanced degree in mathematics. It simply wasn't good enough for me to "trust" my adviser when he or she said my portfolio was doing well. I really needed to be able to judge for myself. I also now knew enough about the world of mutual funds to be sure I didn't want them in my RRSP or non-registered account.

Once I got going I realized a number of other things about myself:

1. I didn't like a lot of buying, selling, and re-buying (i.e., "activity") in my accounts.
2. I didn't want to have to claim capital gains on our non-registered account unless there was a very compelling reason, because that meant paying tax on the gain.
3. I didn't like stocks that were focused in niche markets like uranium processing, or companies with a single product to sell like coffee.
4. I didn't want too much money invested in oil, gas, gold, potash, or other cyclical commodities. Yes, I could have made a bundle buying gold stocks back in 2005 or oil before it hit a hundred dollars a barrel, but I could just as easily have bought gold or oil at its peak and lost money. The problem is—and the research backs me up here—there is no way for the average person to know when gold or anything else is going to go up or down.
5. I wanted companies that produced a reliable dividend and increased it regularly.
6. I wanted a good percentage of my money in bonds or preferred shares that paid a guaranteed return.
7. I wanted the majority of my investments to be in larger companies with long track records.
8. I wanted rock-bottom fees. I was tired of paying fees for services I didn't receive and expertise that turned out to be . . . well, rather less than expert.
9. Above all I wanted my investments to be understandable, so I could easily see how my portfolio was doing without getting a headache. KISS!

....

Capital gains are what you make when you sell an investment for more than you paid for it. The tax on capital gains is lower than the tax on other income, but the gain is still taxed. If you lose money, you have a capital loss to carry forward to other years. That can reduce any tax payable on future capital gains.

....

This makes me seem like such a dull investor. But better dull than desperate! Here's why these things make sense for my husband and me:

- We work for ourselves, so we are more vulnerable than many employees to economic downturns.
- We have no company pension or health plan.
- We take a lot of risks with work and don't need to take more with our money.
- We have a child with a disability and want to be able to help her out if need be.

I came to understand my investment priorities after a period of questioning brought about by dissatisfaction with the way I had allowed my money to be handled. Hard to do at the beginning—especially if you don't have much experience with investments. If you don't know a dividend from a commodity, then how do you decide what you want and what you don't want? The answer is simple: focus on what you do know about yourself. To understand who you are as an investor, you need to think about three main areas: time frame, situation, and risk tolerance (or temperament).

What's Your Time Frame?

Time frame is the easiest aspect of your investor profile to figure out. The bottom line is this: the shorter your time frame—or the sooner you need all or part of your money—the more you need to protect it. This is usually called capital preservation. And the best way to preserve what you've got is to choose investments that don't present a lot of risk.

What does risk have to do with time frame? Let's just say you were investing 100 per cent in equities (stocks themselves or equity mutual funds, which contain stocks), which are riskier than most bonds. Let's assume your investments were worth $250,000 in early 2007 but dropped in value to $150,000 after the market crash of 2008—a typical scenario.

The actual loss is one thing, but the recovery time is another. If your reduced portfolio earned 5 per cent annually from that point on, it would take nearly *eleven years* to get back to where you started assuming a modest inflation rate of 1 per cent. If you don't have those years, you should ensure that your money isn't too heavily invested in the stock market. It's that simple.

> In the last twenty-five years, there have been seven significant market declines and many smaller ones.

Of course, even if the stock market declines precipitously, you haven't technically lost the money until you actually sell. This is the essence of the buy-and-hold philosophy you will hear repeated constantly—if you hang on, you'll be fine. And it's true that over time, the market does go up. However, you don't want your money tied up in the stock market if you're planning to start drawing on the funds for retirement three years hence, or if you know that you'll need $10,000 for your child's university education or $25,000 for a down payment on a house in two years. If you don't think defensively, you may be forced to sell investments at the least convenient and most costly time.

If your time frame is long—fifteen to thirty years before you're going to need the money—you have the time to ride out events like the tech meltdown of 2000 and the financial crisis of 2008. You may still be hurt in the short term, but the knowledge that time is on your side will allow you to sleep a little easier at night. If your timeline is seven to eight years or less, however, you should not be in the stock market at all (or at least the portion of your funds you will be needing should be somewhere safer and more liquid). All you have to do is ask yourself that one simple question: When will I need the money?

You can refine your approach by looking carefully at your timelines and applying them to the realities of the market. Let's say you have a $40,000 RESP for your twelve-year-old daughter invested in equity mutual funds (which invest in stocks). You expect that you will need funds for her university or college studies in seven years time. From roughly this point on, your new contributions should be devoted to something safe and liquid like GICs or bonds, and you should sell a portion of the mutual funds annually; 20 per cent is a good target. Every year you are reducing your exposure to the stock market and increasing your cash and bonds. The bond portion should be short-term, so you are pretty much all in cash by the time junior flies off to higher education.

High-quality bonds (such as those issued by governments and major corporations) offer a virtually guaranteed return. You can lose money if you sell your bonds before their term is up, but on the whole, these are far safer investments than stocks. Consider the following:

WHAT	AVERAGE ANNUAL 3-YEAR RETURN (PER CENT)	AVERAGE ANNUAL 5-YEAR RETURN (PER CENT)	AVERAGE ANNUAL 10-YEAR RETURN (PER CENT)	AVERAGE ANNUAL 20-YEAR RETURN (PER CENT)
Basket of Canadian government and corporate bonds	7.5	7.1	8.2	9.9

Source: Andex Charts, www.andexcharts.com. As of June 2011.

As you can see, there was never a time over the past twenty years when you would have lost money by investing in this basket of Canadian government (federal, provincial, or municipal) and high-quality corporate bonds. The figures assume that you held your bonds until they matured and then rolled them and the accumulated interest over into new bonds.

Now compare the above with equities or stocks:

WHAT	AVERAGE ANNUAL 3-YEAR RETURN (PER CENT)	AVERAGE ANNUAL 5-YEAR RETURN (PER CENT)	AVERAGE ANNUAL 10-YEAR RETURN (PER CENT)	AVERAGE ANNUAL 20-YEAR RETURN (PER CENT)
S&P/TSX Composite (Canada)	0.2	5.7	8	9.4
S&P 500 Index (US)	1.4	0	–1.8	7.8

Source: Andex Charts, www.andexcharts.com. As of June 2011.

The two charts expose the long-standing myth that you must have a sizable investment in the stock market to grow your money. Over the past twenty years, this hasn't really been true. However, because we don't know what will happen in the next twenty years, your best bet is always to invest defensively by having a portion of your money in equities and a portion in high-quality bonds or cash investments like GICs.

One explanatory note is necessary when you're reading these kinds of return charts: they don't take into account adding new money to the investments, such as you would by contributing monthly to an RRSP. The ten-year return, for example, shows you the result of buying a set amount of that particular investment (bonds or stocks) and holding it for ten years. The figure is the return, on average (including dividends or interest), every year for ten years. If you were adding to the investment every year, then the ten-year return would be different.

Back to risk. Everything you invest in—from stocks to bonds to GICs—has risk. The risk of losing money is what we worry about with chancier investments, but with safer vehicles, there is a risk of not making money. Take a look at the chart on page 82 to see the risks inherent in safer investments such as cash and bonds for an RRSP:

INVESTMENT	RISK	REWARD
Money under the mattress	The money won't grow. Smoking in bed presents added danger.	The money is there whenever you need it.
Bank savings account or GICs	The money grows slowly. It may not keep pace with inflation.	Zero risk of loss. (The government guarantees deposits of $100,000 per person and per joint account.) Slight (currently) gain from interest. Money is readily available.
Federal and provincial government bonds	If you sell before the bond matures, you could potentially lose money.	Almost no risk of loss if held to maturity. Higher return over time than GICs or bank savings.
High-quality, or "investment grade," corporate bonds	If you sell before the bond matures, you could lose money. If the company fails, you will lose money.	Higher return than government bonds. Fairly low risk of loss with the highest-quality companies.

If your time frame is long and your money is in GICs, you risk falling behind inflation. Or if you retire early and have to draw on your savings every year, you risk running out of money if the growth rate is too low. On the other hand, there is no risk that you will lose your principal. Remember, you don't know what inflation will be. You don't know what interest rates will be. But if some of your money is in places where the risk of loss is negligible, then you *do* know that you are unlikely to lose it and that your interest payments are secure.

With stocks or equities your time frame is critical because the market goes up and down over time and investors can get trapped in the troughs. If we consider an equity investment to be risky, it is usually because we realize that there is a chance we will lose some or all of the money invested. Investments that have bigger and more frequent ups and downs—technology stocks like Research in Motion, for example—are riskier than investments that tend to be less excitable, such as staid utility companies like Emera (electricity generation and transmission).

The theory is that if you take a bigger chance—that is, you take on more risk—you should enjoy a bigger reward. Those who threw their hats into the technology ring in the mid-1990s were wonderfully rewarded up to 1999. Then they were brutally punished in 2000. That's the downside of the higher risk = higher reward model. Just look at the following charts to see what I mean:

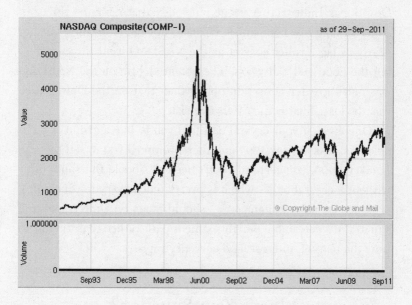

The NASDAQ is a technology-heavy stock index. It went waaay up and then waaay down.

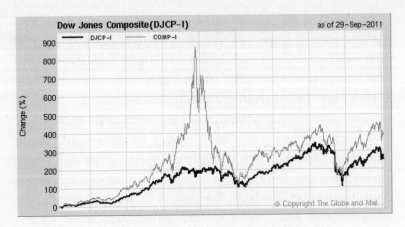

Now look at the bottom line in the graph above. That is the Dow Jones Industrial Average, an index that contains thirty of America's biggest companies. Ups and downs, to be sure, but not nearly as big a roller coaster as the NASDAQ went through during the good and bad years. The potential gain on the NASDAQ was much greater at certain points than that on the Dow, but so was the loss. That is the essence of risk.

Of course, if your crystal ball told you to buy a group of technology stocks in May 1997 and then prompted you to sell them in January 2000, you certainly don't need this book! But those of us without a crystal ball—which is pretty much everyone, including professional money managers—should focus on time frame and situation to determine our investment path rather than trying to time the market, interest, and currency rates.

What's Your Situation?

Situation refers to where you are financially at a given moment and where you expect to be in the future. Someone just starting out as an investor has different needs and a different relationship to risk than someone who is retired on a pension. But that doesn't mean a person just starting out should load up on risk and a retiree should stick with GICs. It all depends on your situation.

$

Case Study: Peter Griffiths, 89, widowed pensioner

My dear old dad has a federal government pension from his twenty-six years in the Canadian Armed Forces. He also has a disability pension from the government because the years of flying thousands of missions and training exercises in the incredibly noisy Argus left him with profound hearing loss. Add in his Old Age Security and his CPP, and my dad, at eighty-nine, is quite comfortable.

He has a small RRIF of $25,000, which he has invested in a variety of stocks over the years. To be clear: he is invested 100 per cent in equities, which is far riskier than investing in something like bonds or GICs. (He does keep sufficient cash on hand to make his required annual withdrawals.) But consider his situation. He doesn't need the money because he has some savings and a very good pension. Losing it would bother him, but it wouldn't materially affect his life (beyond the irritant of his daughter chewing him out for not paying closer attention to her investment advice!).

My father has enjoyed having a small stock portfolio, and his investment choice fits his profile. No, it isn't a great idea for most eighty-nine-year-olds to have everything invested in the stock market. But in his situation it works for him, and for many years he enjoyed following his stocks every morning in the newspaper.

$

Last year, I had a discussion about investments with Moshe Milevsky, one of the new breed of celebrity economists and an associate finance professor at Toronto's York University. When I asked if he invested in bonds, he said, "I am a bond."

"Huh?" I responded.

He explained that since his university defined benefit pension will provide him with a guaranteed return (just like a bond), he doesn't need to buy more for his investment account. Milevsky's situation means that it makes sense for him to ignore bonds and focus on equities. But the pension also means he doesn't have to take on any additional risk unless he wants to.

You may be like me (with no company pension at all) or like my dad and Professor Milevsky (with a guaranteed retirement income). You could also be somewhere in between, with a company-sponsored pension (called a group RRSP or a defined contribution plan), where your employer partially or fully matches your contributions up to a certain amount. Whatever your pension situation, it will have an impact on how you invest your money for retirement.

> Seventy-two per cent of Canadians have no pension plan other than Old Age Security and the Canada Pension Plan, plus whatever savings they have scraped together over the years.

Just a quick word about those group RRSPs or defined contribution (DC) plans, which are the most common non-government pensions for working Canadians. Remember the women in the focus group we met in chapter 3? Several of them contributed to company-sponsored pension plans and had chosen from among a number of investment "packages" presented to them. But like most Canadians, they had only a vague idea of what that package was. None knew their rate of return over time. More critically, most didn't realize that their pension payouts weren't guaranteed in any way, shape, or form. If you participate in a defined contribution plan or group RRSP, it behooves you to be aware of what you have chosen and how it is performing over the years.

Assume you had $250,000 in your company's group RRSP

pension plan in 2008, with an investment mix that was moderate to higher risk (i.e., with more equities or stocks than bonds). Along comes the financial crisis of 2008 and 2009, and suddenly the amount in your pension drops to $200,000. Then let's assume you retired in 2010 at age sixty-five, and on the advice of the company HR person, you moved your pension funds into lower-risk investments such as bonds. Obviously your money would run out much more quickly than if you had been able to hang on to that $250,000 you had in early 2008.

Here's a comparison using a quite conservative 4 per cent annual rate of return. It shows the impact of such a loss.

PENSION AMOUNT	RATE OF RETURN (PER CENT)	MONTHLY WITHDRAWAL	MONEY RUNS OUT IN
$250,000	4	$1,500	20 years
$200,000	4	$1,500	15 years

That lost $50,000 would have a huge effect on the life of a healthy sixty-five-year-old retiree who needs to draw $1,500 a month and has every expectation of living well into his or her eighties.

Interest rates over time are likely to move closer to historical averages (just a guess), so a 6 per cent rate of return may be possible with very safe investments, such as government bonds and cash. If so, here's how things would look:

PENSION AMOUNT	RATE OF RETURN (PER CENT)	MONTHLY WITHDRAWAL	MONEY RUNS OUT IN
$250,000	6	$1,500	30 years
$200,000	6	$1,500	18 years

Knowing what is in your workplace pension and how it is performing is a critical part of your situation. Knowing your time frame with respect to your pension is the other important factor.

But your situation isn't just about pensions. You should also ask yourself questions about where you are now and where you think you might be down the road. Do any of the following statements fit you?

- I work in an industry with low job security.
- I may have to take care of a family member during my retirement.
- I am likely to be single.
- I have health expenses not covered by standard provincial insurance.
- I do not own a home.
- It is important to me to leave as much money as possible to my children.
- I live in an area with high property taxes.
- My home is expensive to maintain.

If you said yes to any of these, you will probably want to consider a lower-risk basket of investments. If you are like my neighbour, who works as a manager in retail sales and has a small group pension at work, you'll probably want to be extra cautious. On the other hand, if you are like my dad or Moshe Milevsky, go ahead and be a day trader, dabble in foreign exchange, or play the options market. Just remember that you don't need to take on risk unless you want to. Your situation, like your time frame, helps determine who you are as an investor.

This brings us to the third factor that determines Who You Are. It is deliberately last on my list, though it is usually first on the list for the financial services industry.

How Much Risk Can You Tolerate? Or, What's Your Investment Temperament?

How much risk can you stomach? This is incredibly tough to figure out. I know, for example, that I am okay on the Ferris wheel but would lose my lunch on the Zipper. My husband isn't okay with either. And I know something else too: I've changed over time. I used to be as daring as Lara Croft, but after my first child was born, I became more vertigo-inclined.

Now, if you've never even been to a fairground, you'd have difficulty deciding which of the rides would suit you. That's how it is with investment risk tolerance too. Risk is all about the chance of losing money—or at least your portfolio losing value—and if you've never had the experience, how do you know how much risk you can tolerate? I've seen very conservative types shrug their shoulders and say, "Oh, well," when the market tanked, taking a good chunk of their savings along with it. And I've also seen market pros, men and women who live on the edge, become physically ill when they lost money in 2000 and 2008.

You can fill out risk tolerance forms until the cows come home, but most people have no idea what their tolerance level really is until they've actually experienced a decline. When my husband and I lost that $30,000 on Royal Trustco back in the early 1990s, I realized that my tolerance for risk was a lot lower than I'd thought. But that doesn't mean I am averse to owning equities. Far from it! I just want the equity part of my portfolio well balanced with bonds and other fixed income to produce a nice guaranteed return. I invest very little of our money in the riskiest sectors, such as mining, precious metals, technology, or commodities. I have also avoided investing in the Far East and so-called emerging markets.

You might think this last decision really limits my potential to make money. After all isn't everyone hollering about how the economic future belongs to countries like China and India? I have no doubt that is true. However, many of the biggest companies in Canada and the United States already earn anywhere from 30 to 70 per cent of their revenues from business conducted in those high-growth areas. I can invest in North American companies and still take advantage of opportunities around the globe.

You can't put a number to your tolerance for risk. And even terms like *low, medium,* and *high* don't really help you match your level of tolerance with a set of investments. That's why I put it on the bottom of my Who You Are list.

Understanding your time frame and your situation is the best way to winnow down the investing options and identify the ones that fit you. Once you've done that, your risk tolerance will help you parcel out your money among the investments (including equities or stocks) that fit your profile.

Above all, my rule about risk tolerance is this: no matter how brave you think you are, cut it in half. It is very easy to be bold in a rising market, but you'll likely feel much different in a falling market. You can always move into riskier, higher-growth investments as you discover an appetite for risk or your situation changes. But it is a real ulcer incubator to go the other way after a crash, when you discover that you're not as risk tolerant as you thought. And as we saw from the charts on pages 80 and 81, and will examine more fully later, loading up on risk doesn't necessarily improve return; in fact, often the opposite is true.

To get you going on your "Who am I?" profile, let's start by looking at mine.

My Investment Profile

Time Frame
- medium
- no plan to draw on my retirement savings for at least ten years

Situation

- no company pension
- self-employed
- one child with a disability who may need some additional financial help
- excellent health (knock on wood)

Risk Tolerance

- medium

And here's what fits my profile:

- larger companies with strong and stable dividends
- as much as 70 per cent invested in equities in the form of exchange-traded funds (I avoid expensive, confusing mutual funds)
- the remainder of my retirement money in bonds in the form of bond exchange-traded funds (as above, I avoid expensive bond mutual funds)

As I get within five years of drawing on my retirement funds, I will be shifting more money into bonds—regardless of interest rates. When I'm sixty-five, I'll have no more than 50 per cent in stocks or exchange-traded funds (ETFs). When I'm seventy, I'll have no more than 30 per cent in stocks or exchange-traded funds. (I'll tell you more about ETFs later.)

Asking yourself the questions posed in this chapter will help you clarify who you are as an investor. Once you have a handle on that—and have read the following chapters—you'll be in a perfect place to understand the group of super-simple portfolios in the final section of the book.

CHAPTER 8

Pick Your Box

I'm moving you slowly and gently toward the comprehensible, easy-to-invest, and low-fee portfolios I'll introduce at the end of the book. I'm also shepherding you in the direction of my Count On Yourself goal, which is to get you completely comfortable with your investments so you can manage them in thirty minutes or less every month.

Even after the previous chapter, you still might not have an accurate fix on your investment profile. That's okay. But I hope you are starting to realize that understanding your time frame, situation, and temperament is a key part of getting your investing house in order.

The next step is to zero in on your accounts themselves. Which ones do you have?

WHAT	YES/NO
Bank savings account	
Tax-free savings account (TFSA)	
Registered education savings plan (RESP)	
Registered disability savings plan (RDSP)	
Registered retirement savings plan (RRSP)	
Registered retirement income fund (RRIF)	
Non-registered investment account	

You may have one, some, or most of the above. As I told Martha Darcy, you should think of these accounts as boxes that are empty when you first open them and then get filled up as you contribute money. Nothing happens to that money until you decide what to do with it. Each box has a unique purpose and a unique time frame; together they dictate your choice of investment products.

Bank Savings Account

Purpose: The best place to hold money to pay for short-term expenditures such as taxes, insurance, and gifts.
Time Frame: Very short to short term (one month to one year).
Appropriate Investments: Cash deposits and short-term GICs (less than one year).

The bank savings box provides the lowest return, but it's also the safest. The Canada Deposit Insurance Corporation (CDIC) protects up to $100,000 of savings in one name and up to $100,000 of savings in joint names.

You won't earn much from deposits in your bank savings account, but it is a convenient holding place. If you don't need access to the money for six to twelve months, you have two options to earn a little more interest.

GICs. These are most commonly available for terms of five years or less. Take care, however, as many GICs are locked in for a specified period. If you cash it in before it comes due, you will lose some or all of the interest. Cashable or redeemable GICs are available, but the interest rate on these is lower.

High-interest savings accounts. Credit unions, virtual and no-frills banks (Achieva, Duca Financial, PC Financial, ING, ICICI), trust companies, and other financial institutions (Canadian Tire

Bank, Dundee Bank of Canada) often offer higher rates for deposits than traditional banks. In some cases, the rates are as good as those you can get on shorter-term GICs. Deposits are insured by either the CDIC or, in the case of credit unions, provincial deposit insurance. If you are in doubt, go to www.cdic.ca for a list of protected institutions or search for "deposit insurance" on your bank or credit union's own website.

We love to hate the banks, mostly because of the high fees and low interest rates. A big part of the Count On Yourself ethos is to check out other options and weigh them carefully. Ten years ago, I saved almost $2,000 in bank fees in a single week. But first I had to get myself—with the help of my friendly neighbourhood bank—into some financial trouble.

.... **$** ....

Case Study: Alison and David, 2001

Many small businesses, contractors, freelancers, and others who are self-employed face an uneven revenue stream. My husband and I are the same; we've always used a credit line to smooth cash flow. It can be difficult for the self-employed to get credit, however, as banks judge what kind of risk you present by looking primarily at your net income. Naturally, like any small business owner, I strive to keep my taxes as low as possible by taking advantage of as many self-employment and small business deductions as I can. This, in turn, lowers my net income, which makes me less attractive to banks.

It all came to a head back in 2001, when our mortgage came due. In the process of renewing it, we were told that the bank's lending policies had been "updated" after the dot-com crash (those looking for credit following the financial crisis heard much the same thing). We'd been dealing with the same bank for fifteen years, had a lot of equity in our home, and could boast a spotless credit rating, but suddenly none of that mattered in the slightest.

The loans officer grandly announced he could squeak us in under the new guidelines for the lowest-rate mortgage, but our $30,000 unsecured credit line had to go. In essence by denying that credit line, the bank forced us to offload what had once been covered by it to, first, a more costly overdraft with fees and, eventually, our even more costly credit cards.

Clever and profitable, at least for the bank.

Interestingly, after refusing the credit line, the bank almost simultaneously increased our overdraft and credit card limits to—you guessed it!—$30,000.

Where once we had a low-interest credit line, suddenly our borrowing attracted fees and high interest payments. Finally, when the interest on and fees for our overdraft, account, and credit card hit $2,000 annually, we got mad as hell and decided not to take it anymore. We moved our accounts to President's Choice Financial, a no-frills bank with kiosks in grocery stores nationwide and an affiliation with CIBC for ATM deposits and withdrawals. As a bonus, PC Financial gave us an unsecured $16,000 credit line at a lower rate than our old one.

"Why doesn't everyone switch from the traditional banks to a no-frills financial institution that will offer more bang for the savings buck?" you ask. Well, the short answer is that it can be a pain. Forms, forms, and more forms, not to mention tax returns and other documents you need to present. What's more, you may be unsatisfied with no-frills banking if you have a business, need a US dollar account or credit cards, or require anything beyond standard bank services. And though many virtual or no-frills banks offer their own RRSP accounts, these may be limited to investments such as GICs. Still, most will allow you to transfer money to or from one of the major banks into your investment account.

We had to retain our business and US dollar accounts at our old bank. Even so, the savings were dramatic, at least $2,000 a year. We diverted these savings into our RRSPs, and after ten years, that money had grown into $26,400. If you take into account the taxes saved with the RRSP contributions, along with the higher interest earned at PC Financial, our $2,000 is worth almost $40,000. Not bad for a week's work.

The Financial Consumer Agency of Canada (accessible online at www.fcac.gc.ca) offers a very cool selector tool to help you sift through various banking options based on your needs. All federally regulated financial institutions are included on the site, though credit unions—which fall under provincial jurisdiction—are not.

Whatever you do with your banking affairs, remember to keep it simple, smarty (KISS). It doesn't make sense to complicate your financial life by opening new accounts just for the sake of a couple of dollars of interest. However, it does make sense to analyze your banking needs, and the fees you're paying, to see if a full or partial switch is in order.

Tax-Free Savings Account (TFSA)

Purpose: Emergency cash or savings for a short- to medium-term goal, such as a car or a home. You can also use a TFSA to shelter investment income from tax. The annual deposit limit is $5,000, but there will likely be increases.
Time Frame: Short to long term (one to twenty-plus years).
Appropriate Investments: Cash deposits, GICs, and short-term bonds.

Our second box is the Tax-Free Savings Account, which is similar to an RRSP in that any investment income, such as interest, dividends, or capital gains, is sheltered from tax. You can also carry your contribution room forward. So if you make no deposit one year, you can contribute $10,000 the next. However, here the similarity to an RRSP ends. You get no tax deduction for contributions, but the money can be withdrawn whenever necessary with no penalty or tax payable. The Canada Revenue Agency describes the TFSA as "an RRSP for everything else in your life."

> Though you can withdraw money from a TFSA at any time, you can replace what you take out only in the next calendar year. If you do, there will be over-contribution penalties. Hopefully, by the time this book is published, this unwieldy and silly rule will have been banished.

Over time your TFSA account could become quite large. Nonetheless, don't be tempted by investments such as equity mutual funds or stocks themselves, unless you are absolutely sure you have no need of the money for at least seven or eight years. Advisers may encourage you to purchase such investment products because the bank makes more money from fees. But most people are better served by GICs or shorter-term bonds in those accounts. These investments provide easy access to your money and a modest rate of return (at least until interest rates rise), and you won't have to worry about selling equity mutual funds during a low point if you have to withdraw some funds.

If your TFSA is multipurpose (emergency funds, short- to medium-term purchases, and a longer-term tax shelter), a good split might be 20 per cent in cash (for emergencies), 30 per cent in a short-term GIC, and 50 per cent in a bond investment (for future purchases and to earn some tax-sheltered income). If you buy individual bonds, treat them and any GICs as "locked-in" investments and plan to hold them for their whole term. If you don't, you could lose interest income or suffer a loss selling the bonds. But if you hold both to maturity, you will get back both your interest income and the amount you originally invested. (I'll explain more about how bonds work in the next chapter.) If, however, your TFSA is just for emergencies and/or a known purchase a year or two hence, keep more in cash and put the rest in short-term GICs.

Despite some cumbersome rules, TFSAs are a welcome addition to your savings plan. Over time they operate as souped-up savings accounts and provide a great place for that all-important emergency cash. If interest rates rise they will become even more beneficial, allowing you to earn tax-sheltered interest income and giving you ready access to the funds without facing withholding tax (as you would when withdrawing money from an RRSP). Just keep in mind the purpose of these accounts, your time frame, and the appropriate investments.

Registered Education Savings Plan (RESP)

Purpose: To help you save for a child's post-secondary education. The cost of a four-year degree is expected to be as much as $100,000 (including living costs) by 2025, so RESPs have never been more important.

Time Frame: Very short to long term—depending on the age of the child.

Appropriate Investments: Bonds, GICs, and equities.

Next up is the box for the Registered Education Savings Plan (RESP). This is a place for parents or other family members to put money aside for a child's education. The beauty of an RESP is that the government gives you twenty cents for every dollar you deposit, up to contributions of $2,500 per year per child, through a program called the Canada Education Savings Grant. (Families with low incomes will get a bit more and those with higher incomes a bit less.) That means the account can grow very quickly, even if the money is just sitting in cash.

Discount or bank brokerages offer simple, easy-to-open
RESP accounts. You can also get group RESP plans,
formerly called scholarship programs. Investigate these
carefully, though; their fees are notoriously high, and the
sales pitches cite questionably high returns.

The important thing to bear in mind with an RESP is that your
investment mix should change as your time frame does. You may
not know exactly when your child will head off to higher education, but you should assume, at least initially, that you will need
to start drawing on the funds when the child turns eighteen. Your
time frame will be long term when your child is a toddler and will
decrease to very short term by the time he or she is seventeen.

RESP rules have become much more flexible in recent years.
The accounts can remain open for far longer. Here's what the
government says: "The plan (RESP) has to be completed (closed)
by the end of the year that includes the 35th anniversary of the
opening of the plan." The funds can also be used for a wide range
of post-secondary options. If one child doesn't study beyond high
school, the money can be transferred to a sibling. You can also
withdraw your contributions tax-free. But note that if you close
the account, you will have to repay the government grant and any
income earned on the grant portion. You may also have to pay tax
on any investment income earned on your contributions. You can
reduce the tax by transferring your contributions and any income
earned into an RRSP if you have contribution room.

Many people start out with 100 per cent of RESP contributions
invested in equities (usually mutual funds), but as the time frame
shortens, you must reduce the percentage in the stock market
and turn to less risky and more liquid investments, such as bonds
and GICs. You will see in later chapters, though, that a portfolio
invested entirely in equities doesn't always outperform a balanced
and less risky portfolio holding cash, bonds, and equities.

I was shocked when I recently canvassed a number of bank advisers for RESP options and none suggested investing in either GICs or bonds. Even worse, not one advised switching to bonds and GICs when the child reached thirteen (or at any other age, for that matter). All of them recommended mutual funds, which of course generate higher fees. Recently banks have begun advocating a new product called Target Date funds, which hold a basket of other mutual funds. These do alter the investment mix as you get closer to needing the money (that's the "target date" part), but many of them have high fees and offer only mediocre performance, so you have to research them carefully.

There can be serious pitfalls if you don't move to safer, more liquid investments as your child gets closer to college age.

$

Case Study: Maja, 46, and William, 48

For years, Maja and William, a bookkeeper and a transit driver, socked away money in an RESP for their twins, Jeff and Jamie, investing in three equity (stock) mutual funds recommended by their bank's adviser years earlier. In 2008, just as the two boys set off to university, the market crashed in the wake of the subprime mortgage mess. The mutual funds took a shellacking, losing 40 per cent on average. The value of their RESP dropped from about $60,000 to just over $36,000. Because Maja and William didn't want to sell the mutual funds at a loss, they took out a home equity line of credit to pay for the nearly $20,000 in tuition fees, residence costs, and other expenses.

As I write this in mid-2011, their RESP sits at $51,000, still about 15 per cent below what it was in 2007. Hoping to completely recoup their money, Maja and William still haven't sold any units or withdrawn any funds from the RESP. But Jamie is now just a semester from graduation, and Jeff dropped out after two years. At this point, neither wants to pursue more education.

$

In Maja and William's case, the RESP can remain in place until they are required by the government to collapse it. But if they had started moving their RESP toward cash and bonds when the boys were thirteen, they wouldn't have been squeezed when the market collapsed. Not only have they lost money as a result, but they've wasted time and effort and taken on a lot of stress worrying about their investments and what to do with them.

> You can get information about RESPs, from how to open one to what happens if the plan is collapsed, on the government website www.canlearn.ca.

Mutual funds (equity, bond, or money market) are the most common investments for RESPs. I don't like them generally, but I particularly don't like them for RESPs. They are expensive and confusing, and it's really, really tough to pick good ones. However, mutual funds can be purchased in small amounts monthly with automatic debits from your account and no trading commission, making them very convenient. But you end up paying dearly for that convenience with management and sales fees. The deferred sales charges also make it more difficult to move from equities to cash at the appropriate time.

I also don't generally recommend buying individual stocks for RESPs—your job is to protect the money for your child's education—but if you are confident picking stocks or are fortunate enough to have a skilled and knowledgeable adviser, go for it. Exchange-traded funds (ETFs) or index mutual funds are my choice for the equity portion of an RESP for most people, and I'll be detailing them fully as this book unfolds.

However, even if you just stick with bonds and GICs for an RESP, you will do very nicely over time. You already have a wonderful return on your investment because of that twenty cents on the dollar you're getting from the government. That's free money. Easy money. Take it and don't risk it on questionable mutual funds recommended by a salesperson (with the emphasis on sales).

Here's how your RESP will grow if you contribute $2,500 per year to get the maximum education savings grant:

TYPE OF INVESTMENT	YOUR CONTRIBU-TION	GOVERN-MENT GRANT	RATE OF RETURN OVER TIME (PER CENT)	VALUE AFTER TEN YEARS	VALUE AFTER EIGH-TEEN YEARS
GICs	$2,500 a year ($208.33 a month)	$500 a year ($41.67 a month)	4	$37,000	$79,000
Mix of bonds and GICs	$2,500 a year ($208.33 a month)	$500 a year ($41.67 a month)	5	$39,000	$87,000
Mix of bonds and equities up to age thirteen; mix of bonds and GICs thereafter	$2,500 a year ($208.33 a month)	$500 a year ($41.67 a month)	7 to age thirteen; 5 there-after	$43,000	$98,000

In this chart, I have used a conservative rate of return. You might do much better if interest rates rise or the stock market continues its current strong performance. The difference between the mix of bonds and GICs and the less conservative mix of bonds and equities is about $11,000 over eighteen years. That's not peanuts, but it's a lot less than you might have imagined for the absolute security and flexibility of your money.

If you choose to invest some money in the stock market (with mutual funds, exchange-traded funds, or index mutual funds), I advise you to start switching to something more conservative when your child reaches thirteen. (In the final chapters of the book I'll introduce you to index mutual funds, which are a cross between ETFs and mutual funds.) Since you'll have only five or six years left until you may need to withdraw the funds, your goal is to protect the money. The last thing you want to be faced with is a fat tuition bill, and no cash available, during a market meltdown.

But what happens if your child turns thirteen just as the market tanks, and you're already heavily invested in equity mutual funds? Your best strategy in that situation is to funnel all new contributions into short-term bonds (such as a bond ETF) or cash and to sell 10 per cent of your mutual funds each year, regardless of the hit you may take. (That way at least you won't trigger deferred sales charge fees, which are attached to many mutual funds if you sell them within six years of purchase.)

Yes, if you did this between 2007 and mid-2008, you would have sold into a falling market. But you would have been selling into a rising market throughout 2009 and 2010. In the end, you might have lost some money, but it would have cost you less than being forced to sell a large portion of your funds at the worst point in a market meltdown.

One final note about RESPs: many parents find it extremely difficult to contribute $2,500 annually, per child, to an education savings plan and still contribute to their own RRSPs. I believe it will become increasingly common over the next few decades for youngsters to work for a year or two before university or college, and I think this is an excellent idea. Many young people are not ready for the hallowed halls of academe at eighteen, or they don't really know what they want to do or study. It is a particularly brilliant strategy if your child is interested in one of the trades or a specific profession. A period of time working in the field can focus or deflect his or her interest.

At the very least, ensure that your children start contributing to their own RESPs with a portion of their income as they enter the teen years.

Case Study: Quinn Cruise, 25

Quinn worked during the summer from the time she was fourteen and had a few part-time jobs during the school year. We agreed that she would put 25 per cent of her part-time income and 50 per cent of summer income in the RESP, and she was thrilled when the government topped up her contributions by 20 per cent. By the time she headed off to university, she had contributed almost $8,000 to her own education.

Quinn then spent four years studying to become an environmental scientist. But after working in a testing lab one summer, she decided she hated the part of the profession that can be tedious to those with—as she put it—a "restless" personality.

Interestingly, she ended up in another lab, of sorts—a kitchen. As I write this, she is learning how to make aioli from scratch in a two-year chef's training program at George Brown College in Toronto. It's all science in the end, but for her, the creativity of the kitchen is a better fit.

You can come up with the percentage contribution that makes sense for you, but I guarantee that your children will get engaged with the process. When they're in their mid-teens, they may not completely appreciate what they are doing or why, but when they are rocketing down the post-secondary road, they will feel great pride in having had a financial hand in their future.

Registered Disability Savings Plan (RDSP)

Purpose: A substitute for (or an addition to) an RRSP for a person with a disability.

Time Frame: Medium to very long (ten-plus years).

Appropriate Investments: Cash deposits, GICs, bonds, and equities.

Registered Disability Savings Plans (RDSPs) are relatively new on the investment scene. They operate like a cross between an RESP and an RRSP, in that you make annual contributions and the government tops them up with a grant portion (both of which can be carried forward to future years). There are also rules for withdrawals—the key one being that funds must remain in the account for ten years before anything can be withdrawn tax-free. (The formula for withdrawals is a bit complex but hopefully will be simplified as these plans mature.) Depending on the person's income and contributions, the grant portion can add as much as $4,500 annually.

Like all registered accounts, RDSPs shelter any income earned from tax. But there is no tax deduction for contributions. To open an RDSP, a child or adult must first have applied for and received a disability tax credit certificate.

> The Canada Revenue Agency site (www.cra-arc.gc.ca) explains who is eligible for the disability tax credit and how to apply for it. Type the phrase "disability tax credit" into the search window. Or go to www.rdsp.com to learn more.

Registered Retirement Savings Plan (RRSP)

Purpose: To support us during our golden years!

Time Frame: Very short to very long.

Appropriate Investments: Cash, bonds, and equities.

Our next box is the one most familiar to Canadians—the Registered Retirement Savings Plan, or RRSP. (Repeat after me: "This is just a box. This is just a box.") Many people have great anxiety over their RRSPs because they have no idea what to invest in, and when they do invest they can't figure out how well they're doing. The financial services industry aggressively sells thousands of mutual funds and other products for RRSP investments, making staggering sums on fees and sales commissions. Some of these products are very good, but far too many are expensive and produce only mediocre returns.

As with other investment accounts, time frame is the key factor in determining what investments you choose for your RRSP. When you're twenty-five or thirty, your time frame seems endless; when you're sixty, not so much. My rule about taking on less risk as your time frame shortens operates exactly the same way here as it does with RESPs. Your investment mix should change as you move toward your retirement years, when you will start withdrawing the money.

But if less time means you should take on less investment risk, surely the opposite must also be true—with more time, you should be able to take on more investment risk.

Yes, that can certainly be the case. But it doesn't have to be.

The financial services industry says: "If you have a long time frame, you can afford to take some risks." But I say, "If you have a long time frame, you don't *need* to take risks." In fact, if you choose a more conservative route, you likely will end up at your retirement destination more safely and just as quickly. My advice is not to get sucked into riskier investments just because you have twenty-five or thirty years until retirement. Twenty years ago, everyone was hollering about equities. "You can't get rich if you don't invest in the stock market!" was the industry chorus. The underlying message was that you were wasting your money if you put it into bonds, money market accounts, or GICs. And we Canadians listened, obediently pouring billions into mutual funds, paying exorbitant management fees as we went.

Twenty years down the road were we better off than those who'd stuck to less risky stuff? Take a look and see:

	GOVERNMENT AND HIGH-QUALITY CORPORATE BONDS (PER CENT)	US AND CANADIAN LARGER COMPANY STOCKS (PER CENT)
Rate of Return 1991–2011*	9.9	8.6

*The bond mix is 50–50 government and corporate. The stock mix is 50–50 United States and Canada. Interest income and dividends have been reinvested.

If you had purchased boring old bonds over this time period and kept rolling them over as they came due, your return would be higher than that earned by those who put the same amount of money into the stock market. The reason for this startling difference is that the stock market has suffered numerous setbacks since 1990, and most especially since 2000. And as we've seen, it takes many years to recover from big losses. On the other hand, bonds (assuming you hold them to maturity) keep producing a positive return year in and year out.

Now, I'm not saying that you should rush off and sell all your equity mutual funds or stocks because the rates of return from 2010 to 2030 will match what we saw from 1990 to 2010. No one knows what will happen in the next twenty years, just as no one knew what was going to happen twenty years ago, when most experts were heralding equities. But there are some things we do know:

- Certain investments, such as bonds and GICs, offer a guaranteed, or highly safe, rate of return.
- Market swings can be sudden and vicious.
- It can take years and years to recover from losses, and those with poorly designed portfolios and high-fee mutual funds will lose even more during market downturns and recover more slowly during upturns.
- Short time frames demand that you be very conservative with your capital.

- Longer time frames give you a better chance of riding out gyrations in the market.
- The magic of compounding (interest earning interest over time) means you can still do quite nicely with a conservative mix.

The secret, as you'll see in the coming chapters, is to have a balanced, low-fee, and simple RRSP portfolio that meets your specific needs.

Registered Retirement Income Fund (RRIF)

Purpose: To provide an annual income in retirement.
Time Frame: Short to long (depends on your longevity genes!).
Appropriate Investments: Cash, bonds, and equities.

By the end of year you turn seventy-one, you are required to transfer your RRSP to a Registered Retirement Income Fund (RRIF), and the following year you must begin making mandatory withdrawals. This is a straightforward process your financial institution can help you with. Although RRIFs are for your later years, you should treat them much like RESPs, which belong in life's early years. Since you must withdraw a required amount every year after age seventy-one (much like an RESP, where you withdraw money annually to pay education costs), you need to make sure your portfolio is constructed so there is enough cash available to make those withdrawals. Sadly, many RRIFs are not well set up, and in 2008 and 2009 I saw many retirees having to sell equity mutual funds at huge losses in order to make the mandatory withdrawal.

Depending on your situation, an RRSP could certainly be invested 100 per cent in equities, as my dad's was before and after he converted to a RRIF. But most people will need to start moving funds into more liquid investments so that they don't get stuck selling at a market low point. I recommend having at least three years' worth of RRIF withdrawals in cash (GICs are fine). That way you never have to worry.

Non-registered Investment Account

Purpose: To save and invest outside an RRSP.
Time Frame: Medium to very long.
Appropriate Investments: Cash, bonds, and equities.

Because the majority of Canadians struggle to maximize their RRSP contributions, non-registered investment accounts are not as common. However, there are some advantages to saving and investing in a non-registered account as well as—or in some cases, instead of—an RRSP. Those advantages are as follows:

- You can get at the money at any time without paying tax as you would if you had to withdraw funds from an RRSP.
- Those with higher retirement incomes might avoid clawback of government benefits, since money taken out of a non-registered account is not added to income as a RRIF or RRSP withdrawal is.
- Those with low incomes who are eligible for the Guaranteed Income Supplement (GIS) might be better off with a non-registered account since every dollar of withdrawal from an RRSP counts as income and may reduce GIS payments (depending, of course, on your income level).

Many people open non-registered accounts to play the market. But research shows that frequent traders who buy and sell stocks or bonds almost without exception do far worse than those who plot a steadier course.

Now that I have explained the various boxes, or investment accounts, it is time for you to decide how you should divvy up your deposits and contributions.

CHAPTER 9

Spread Your Eggs

My granny knew. "Don't put all your eggs in one basket," she'd say. "Spread them around. If one basket falls, you won't break all your eggs." Granny's advice works brilliantly as an investment tool. In fact, along with keeping things simple, this is the most powerful bit of advice I have to impart. If you do only those two things with your investments, you'll do fine.

Believe it or not, what my granny knew about eggs won Dr. Harry Markowitz a Nobel Prize in Economics in 1990. He was awarded the coveted honour after thirty-two years of research into what he called modern portfolio theory. Markowitz was able to prove with complex mathematical modelling that diversifying your investments maximizes return over time and minimizes risk. Or put in my granny's words, he showed that you shouldn't put all your investment eggs in one basket. The bonus to spreading your eggs around is that it will actually improve your return while it decreases the risk. Now that's a neat trick!

How you do this is actually quite easy, but it doesn't have a comfortable or huggable name—it's called asset allocation. If you say it aloud a couple of times, it doesn't seem as ominous!

Assets are your eggs (money).

Allocation is the practice of spreading them around.

Before you can make a decision about where you want to put your investment dollars, you need to be aware of the options.

There are three major baskets, or asset classes: cash, fixed income, and equities. I've talked about these baskets earlier, but let's look at them in more detail.

Cash

The cash basket is sometimes lumped in with fixed income, but I am going to keep them separate for now. Cash includes bank savings, GICs, and Canada Savings Bonds (which, despite their name, are closer to the cash asset class than they are to bonds). As we've already discussed, this is the safest asset class with the lowest rate of return. But don't diss cash investments. Over the last twenty years, five-year GICs would have earned you 4.5 per cent annually if you'd reinvested the interest and rolled over the GIC when it came due.

"Aha!" you say. "But that included the years of double-digit interest rates, when you could retire at forty-five because you were getting an 18 per cent return on GICs."

Actually, no. Except for the early years of the 1990s (when rates averaged more than 8 per cent) and the years following the subprime mortgage fiasco (when the prime sunk to 2.25 per cent), the prime rate has bounced around in the 5.5 to 6.75 per cent range. Even though there were three years when five-year GICs would have returned 2 per cent or less, you still would have averaged a return of 4.5 per cent over the past twenty years just from this cash investment. I can tell you that many people who were predominantly invested in the stock market over the same period would have been delighted with that kind of return.

Over the most recent ten years, of course, the return for cash doesn't look so good. If you had invested in five-year GICs from 2001 to 2011, you would have earned about 3.5 per cent, assuming you rolled the GIC over into a new one when it came due and reinvested the interest.

But here's the point: if you had put your investment eggs into this basket, you would NEVER have broken a single egg. Not one. Even though the cash asset class is sneered at in these days of ultra-low interest rates, GICs are still the most wonderful things in the entire world when you need safety. Best of all, they require almost no care or attention. There's something to be said for that kind of relationship.

Still, as safe as cash is, there are risks—especially if you violate the "eggs in one basket" principle.

Cash Risk 1: Opportunity Cost

If you lock in GICs at low rates for a long time period, you lose the ability to switch to ones offering a higher return when rates rise. This risk is called opportunity cost (or sometimes, interest rate risk). But many investors lock in for long periods to get a slightly higher return because that return is sufficient for their needs, and they'd rather have the certainty than worry about what will happen in the future. I have no problem with someone making an informed decision like that; it shows she knows who she is as an investor.

Case Study: Marjorie, 61, retired

I met Marjorie in 2010 at a seminar in Baddeck, on Cape Breton Island, one of my favourite places in the world. Talk about what money can't buy! The Bras D'Or Lakes are truly golden when the light is right. The crackle and thunder of the northern lights at Ingonish Beach seem to take you right into the heart of heaven—no ticket required.

Marjorie had worked for most of her life on the phone, dispatching taxis and trucks, organizing school bus routes, and placing orders for a mining supplier. Her income never rose above $32,000 in thirty-five years. But today Marjorie is happy and secure. And this is how she got there.

"My mother told me that you never know what is going to happen in life, so you always have to put something away just in case," she told me. "I started putting a few dollars aside when I got my first job at eighteen. I have done that every year since.

"I didn't know anything about investing, but when I was in my forties I asked an adviser to put my money somewhere very, very safe. I told him I didn't want to put anything in the stock market. I never wanted to take any chances. It would have been nice to make millions, but it was more important to me that my money was safe.

"I just retired a year ago and I never had a company pension, but my money is there for me and it's enough for me to live the kind of life I want. Life is good!"

$

Marjorie is a poster girl for Count On Yourself. She did almost everything right, but she was wrong about one thing: she underestimated herself when she said she didn't know anything about investing. Okay, maybe she had never met a naked short and wouldn't know an option from a maple tree. But Marjorie knew *herself,* and her conservative GIC and bond portfolio suited her perfectly.

You can avoid opportunity cost these days by holding short-term GICs (which will pay you less than longer-term ones), or by doing what Marjorie's adviser did, buying multiple GICs with different terms: ninety days, six months, one year, and so on. This is called laddering. Laddering allows you to put some of your money to work at a better return if rates rise while still benefiting from the higher rates on medium- and longer-term GICs. But for most people, especially now that rates are more likely to go up than down, a single short-term GIC will suffice.

Cash Risk 2: Too Many Eggs in the Cash Basket

This second scenario may never happen again, but it's worth being aware of all the same. In the early 1980s, soaring interest rates caused a stampede into cash investments such as GICs and T-bills. In those days, even short-term GICs were earning 15 to 18 per cent. It seemed that the era of high interest rates, created by the government to fight inflation, would never end.

But of course, it did end. The prime rate peaked in 1981 at 22.75 per cent, then eighteen short months later, rates had dropped by half. Still high by today's standards, but a disaster for those who bet the farm on rates staying in the stratosphere.

I knew several people who were crowing about their income bonanza after they'd converted their stocks or mutual fund portfolios entirely into cash investments. Some even retired early based on the flow of dough. But when rates dropped, they were left with insufficient income. Even worse, by the time they got around to shifting some of their investments back to equities, the market had taken off and they'd missed most of the ride up.

The lessons are simple: Don't ignore an asset class like cash just because the returns are currently low. And don't be tempted to put too many eggs in a single basket because that asset class happens to be booming.

How to Invest in Cash

The three most common ways to invest in cash are bank or high-interest savings accounts, GICs, and money market mutual funds.

High-interest (a bit of an oxymoron these days) savings accounts are flexible and very useful for short- to medium-term savings. If you have cash in your RRSP, you are better off buying a GIC; most RRSP accounts pay only minimal interest on cash and don't offer any "high-interest option." There are RRSP accounts just for cash, often called RRSP savings accounts, and these do pay a higher rate of return. But if you choose this route, you will end up with two accounts—one for cash and one for your other investments, which of course violates my KISS principle. So think carefully before you do it.

The downside to holding a GIC in an RRSP is that most brokerages have minimum purchase amounts, often $5,000, which doesn't work for those just starting out and contributing small amounts. If this is you, you can collapse cash and bonds into your fixed income basket for a few years. I'll deal with the issue of cash for beginning or smaller accounts in more detail later.

Money market mutual funds, which invest in GICs, T-bills, and other "cash equivalents," are available from virtually every fund company out there. They used to be a great place to hold money for the short term or to invest long term in cash. But in these days of low interest rates, the fees on money market accounts eat up most of your meagre return, so you are better off avoiding them.

Fixed Income

Our second basket, or asset class, is fixed income. The main fixed income investment is bonds. (There are others, such as debentures and mortgage-backed securities, but bonds are more accessible and suit most people.) There's a big wide world of them available, from ultra-safe government bonds, to those issued by corporations, to some really, really risky investments called junk bonds. As the name suggests, these bonds have a greater chance of not only breaking your investment eggs but pulverizing them—if you bet . . . er, invest wrong. But junk bonds do pay a higher rate of interest, to compensate for their considerable risk. If you want to investigate the world of these bonds, you can certainly do so. But I'm not going to cover them in this book.

Bonds have a face value that shows how much they are worth at maturity and they pay a stated rate of return for a specific period of time (ranging from one to thirty years). They can also be bought and sold. Bond traders make money on the difference between purchase and sale. Though bonds are considered pretty dull investments, the world of bond trading is actually fast-paced and not for the faint of heart.

Over time, investment-quality bonds (government bonds and those issued by stable corporations) have returned between 6 and 10 per cent annually on average—that is, if you hang on to them until maturity, then roll them over with the reinvested interest. As I write this, however, a Government of Ontario bond that matures (or comes due) in five years is offering a paltry 2.5 per cent return. Still, you shouldn't ignore bonds just because the return is low at a given time. They are safe if you stick with the government and high-quality corporate versions. And if you invest in shorter-term bonds, you can roll them over into ones with a higher return when rates rise.

How to Invest in Bonds

There are four ways most investors buy bonds for their portfolios: retail bonds, bond mutual funds, bond exchange-traded funds, and bond index mutual funds.

Buying bonds on a retail or individual basis is the way our parents used to do it. That Government of Ontario bond I just mentioned is a retail bond, and it can be purchased with various maturity dates and for various amounts. If you already have a brokerage account for your RRSP or other investments, go to the Fixed Income tab on your account page to see a list of bonds available for purchase that day and their maturity dates. Note there is a fee attached to buying bonds, but you won't actually see it because it's embedded in the price. (There's no free lunch anywhere!) Generally you need to have $10,000 or more to get the best price on retail bonds.

All bonds have a face value and an interest rate coupon. The interest payment you get from a bond is called the yield, and it changes with the price. For example, if you buy a bond with a face value of $5,000 and a 5 per cent interest rate coupon, your yield is 5 per cent. You would receive $250 annually for the term of the bond. But if interest rates take a jump, the value of that bond will decline because the yield is less appealing. If you bought that bond for $4,500 with the same 5 per cent coupon attached, your yield from interest would be 5.5 per cent plus the $500 capital gain when the $5,000 bond matures. That $500 profit, when averaged out over the term of the bond, boosts your yield slightly beyond the interest coupon. If, on the other hand, you had to pay more than the face value of the bond because interest rates have dropped and the coupon becomes more appealing, your yield will be less than 5 per cent.

Retail bonds can also be purchased as strip bonds. With these, the interest coupon is stripped away and sold to someone else. You buy the bond at a discount because there is no interest paid. But you make money (the yield) on the difference between what you paid for the bond and its face value at maturity. Strip bonds can be handy for those who want to invest in bonds but don't have sufficient funds to buy them with the interest coupon attached. They work best when interest rates are higher. Right now, it won't cost you much more to buy a regular retail bond (especially those with shorter maturities) than a strip bond.

A second way to buy bonds is through bond mutual funds. These are funds that invest in (hold) a variety of bonds. Mutual funds managers trade bonds (buy and sell), searching for the best yields and hoping to make a capital gain when they buy a bond at one price and then sell it at a higher one. The theory behind bond funds used to be sound. A fund manager who has millions to invest can get far better deals than you and I with our few thousand bucks. But today the fees on mutual funds carve a big hole in your return. Also, there are good, bad, and really ugly bond mutual funds, and it can be difficult to know which is which. Most bond managers made piles of money in the last ten years selling bonds as interest rates plummeted, so if you look at the three-, five-, and ten-year returns, they are fantastic. But that was then and this is now. You are unlikely to get those same returns with those same bond funds if and when interest rates rise and fund managers are forced to replace maturing bonds with ones offering a far lower yield. So don't be fooled by history.

Fortunately, there is a better and cheaper alternative to either retail bonds or bond mutual funds.

Exchange-traded funds (ETFs) are my absolute favourite way to buy bonds. Bond ETFs simply hold a basket of bonds that mirror a given bond index. Just as the Dow Jones Industrial Average tracks the performance of thirty of America's largest companies, bond indices track the performance of various types of bonds. There are government and corporate bond indices, as well as indices that contain global or US bonds. For most of the major bond indices, there is a bond ETF that can be purchased by any investor.

When you buy units of a bond ETF, you are simply purchasing a small piece of the index. You buy the units exactly as you would purchase shares in a bank or any other listed company. Of course, you will pay a trading fee, but—good news again!—trading fees at discount brokerages have plummeted thanks to increasing competition.

I love bond ETFs because the management fees are tiny, as they are for most ETFs. There is no manager or research team to pay, no buying and selling. Bond ETFs simply follow a given index. When we get to the next section, Take Action, I will show you the best bond ETFs for most investors. Lovely creatures, those bond ETFs, and so user-friendly.

There is also a cousin to bond ETFs called bond index mutual funds. These do exactly what bond ETFs do, but they are mutual funds (which means there is usually no fee to buy, though sometimes you will pay to sell). The MERs are higher for these funds than bond ETFs but lower than regular mutual funds because there is no buying or selling. They are a good, low-fee alternative if you have small amounts to invest monthly, especially if you don't qualify for lower trading fees at your brokerage.

Equities

I've saved the biggest basket, or asset class, for last. Equities are those tens of thousands of stocks you can buy through any discount or full-service broker. You can buy stock in big companies and small ones, in companies at home and abroad. There are companies digging holes in the ground and others digging into cyberspace. There are so-called bricks-and-mortar companies you see every day (banks, department stores, grocery stores) and companies whose products you never actually see at all because they are buried deep underground or are simply too small to see without a microscope. In short, there are companies (stocks) to fit every interest, budget, and investment style.

Equities are usually purchased as either common stock or preferred shares. Preferred shares are equities, but they behave a bit like bonds, in that they pay a set amount called a dividend (most preferred shares issue payments quarterly). They usually trade in a narrow range and are most commonly issued at $25 a share, though $50 and $100 preferred shares do exist. There is still some risk of loss, just as there is with stocks, because companies do fail. (Remember our experience with Royal Trustco.) Also, the price is not guaranteed. During the financial crisis, for example, the preferred shares of many banks and real estate companies dropped as low as $13. Still, high-quality preferred shares are handy additions to the portfolios of income-oriented investors and retirees because the rate of return is known and usually fairly secure.

Equities (common stock) can be very volatile. You have the opportunity to achieve tremendous gains if you pick your investments well (and have lady luck on your side), but you can also lose the most with this asset class because it is the one most vulnerable to a stumble or a flat-out face plant. And certain sectors of the stock market fall more often and more sharply than others. Still, this is the asset class where most people want to put some of their investment eggs, not only because of the growth potential but also because of the dividends. Many companies pay dividends to shareholders on common stock, and if you invest in companies that raise their dividends regularly, it adds the same kind of ballast to your portfolio as interest payments on bonds and cash.

How to Invest in Equities

There are four ways you can invest in equities: individual stocks or shares, mutual funds, exchange-traded funds, and index mutual funds.

Stocks (both common and preferred) of individual companies can be purchased on stock exchanges. What keeps many people from buying stocks is the difficulty in picking a well-balanced and diversified portfolio. It is extremely dangerous to invest in only a handful of stocks or to follow the latest hot tip. You need fifteen to twenty-five stocks spread across various sectors to keep your risk of loss as low as possible. Loading up on one stock or sector—as many people did during the tech boom of 1995–2000 and the financial and real estate bubbles of 2004–2008—is a recipe for disaster. It's that "too many eggs in too few baskets" issue.

Another deterrent to buying stocks is the expense. Even with today's discounted trading fees, you can run up quite a bill assembling a stock portfolio and adding to it over time. The best way to protect yourself against market dips and outright meltdowns is to buy regularly—this is called dollar cost averaging. But if you do this, the costs can really add up with a twenty-stock portfolio, even if you just add to it or rebalance it twice a year.

Rebalancing, or portfolio housekeeping, which we'll discuss in detail later, is critical to managing a stock portfolio. If you are a DIYer, it is all too easy to let a handful of stocks dominate in a strong market. That's what happened to many investors prior to the dot-com bust. If you had been pruning Nortel as the stock price rose, to keep it in proportion to the other stocks in your portfolio, you would have been protecting yourself against the fall. I had a similar experience with Bombardier in my early investing years. It escalated from about 6 per cent of my portfolio to 32 per cent. I was so delighted with the increasing value, I just let it grow and grow. Then it hit the dirt, dropping from nearly $17 a share in 2002 to less than $4 in 2003. I still made money, but not as much as I would have if I'd pruned it periodically.

Most people buy equities the second way, in the form of equity mutual funds that invest in stocks. But there can be a lot of buying and selling (called turnover) in mutual funds as the manager attempts to get the best return and outperform competing funds. Believe it or not, these managers fall into the same traps that regular investors do—bad stock picking, poor timing, and out-and-out wrong guesses about which way the market or a particular company is going.

These days there are so many mutual funds—somewhere around fifteen thousand of them!—that it is extremely difficult to pick good ones that will remain solid over time. And because the industry is based on fees, the business has become all about selling. Worst of all, those high fees erode your profits.

The best way to buy equities for your portfolio is the third way. Exchange-traded funds, with their tiny fees, produce a much better result for most people. They are listed on stock exchanges, just like stocks, and because you are buying a piece of a given index, rather than paying a manager to try to outperform the market, they offer higher and more reliable returns over time. ETFs are the basis of the portfolios I am going to lay out at the end of the book. (I will introduce index mutual funds as an alternative to ETFs in the final chapters.)

Now that you know a bit about the main investment baskets, or asset classes, let's start to make some decisions about how to parcel out your eggs among them.

CHAPTER 10

How Many Investment Eggs in Which Baskets?

In the previous chapter I focused on the three main baskets, or asset classes: cash, fixed income, and equities. But what percentage of your investment eggs should you put in each of those baskets? And how do you make that decision?

Both questions are vitally important to you as an investor. Believe it or not, the way you spread your investment eggs—and how diligently you stick to that decision—will have a bigger impact on your return than picking the right stocks or mutual funds. In other words, the housekeeping part of investing is paramount to how well your portfolio performs over time.

This is a fact rarely mentioned when you sign up for investment advisory services. You will hear about the high-quality mutual funds the firm seeks out. You'll hear about the advantages of this style versus that style of investing and how the adviser and/or firm has a technique for selecting only the best funds for your portfolio. From advisers and brokers who manage stock portfolios, you'll hear some version of "We've got a primo research team that unearths undervalued companies around the globe." (Whenever I hear this last pronouncement, I always have an image of these undervalued companies infested with researchers, to the point that they can't get any work done.) However, you rarely hear anything about the very simple housekeeping that keeps your portfolio healthy.

The truth is, the industry doesn't really want you to know that one of the most important aspects of portfolio management is easily within the capabilities of the average person with half an hour to devote to the task each month—assuming you have a simple portfolio. (Apologies to my professional investment friends, but it's true!) Wealth managers tell me privately that over time 60 per cent or more of the money they make for clients comes from the discipline of selecting an asset allocation, maintaining it through the ups and downs of stock markets and interest rates, and reinvesting dividends and interest income.

If you choose to put 50 per cent of your portfolio in bonds and 50 per cent in equities (stocks, mutual funds, or ETFs), then your housekeeping job is to examine that allocation from time to time and either add to your investments with new contributions or sell a portion of the asset that is booming and buy more of the one that is sagging. This is called rebalancing, and together with reinvesting dividends and interest income, it is the foundation of any strong portfolio.

> The foundation of successful investing is portfolio house-keeping, not—I repeat not—buying and selling, timing the market, or having access to crack research teams.

Case Study: Carla, 43, mine manager

Carla, the single parent of a fifteen-year-old, is a diligent saver with an RRSP valued at $160,000. In her early years, she relied on a bank adviser who loaded her up with a slew of mutual funds. But apart from her monthly contributions, her RRSP investments hardly grew.

Frustrated, Carla decided to strike out on her own. She sold her mutual funds, even though she had to pay deferred sales charges averaging between 2 to 4 per cent, to begin again with a strategy of investing in the North American stock market, concentrating on what she knows. Because Carla works in the technology field and started her career in mine operation logistics, she is comfortable with the language of those fields and invests heavily in mining and related technology. She's also a fan of the financial services sector, and has about 25 per cent of her investments in Canadian banks and other financial stocks.

$

Carla is a very aggressive investor with most of her money in equities. At last glance, her asset allocation looked like this:

- Cash—3 to 15 per cent (depending on her buying and selling of stocks)
- Bonds—None
- Equities (stocks)—85 to 97 per cent (60 per cent Canadian, 40 per cent US)

She owns anywhere from eighteen to twenty-five stocks at one time. Some (like the banks) she hangs on to for the long term; others she buys and sells depending on what's happening in the sector and in the economy.

Here's how the return of Carla's portfolio looked in June 2011 compared to the return of the broader Canadian and US markets:

	CARLA'S RRSP AVERAGE ANNUAL RETURN (PER CENT)	S&P/TSX COMPOSITE INDEX (CANADIAN) TOTAL RETURN (PER CENT)	S&P 500 INDEX (US) TOTAL RETURN (PER CENT)
1 year	19	20.9	18.4
3 years	0.3	0.2	1.4

	CARLA'S RRSP AVERAGE ANNUAL RETURN (PER CENT)	S&P/TSX COMPOSITE INDEX (CANADIAN) TOTAL RETURN (PER CENT)	S&P 500 INDEX (US) TOTAL RETURN (PER CENT)
5 years	4.2	5.7	0
10 years	5.3	8	−1.8

Total return is the combination of stock price growth (or decline) and dividends.

Overall, Carla has done remarkably well, even with a large portion of her portfolio in the sad-sack US stock market.

These figures also take into account Carla's trading fees. Because her account has more than $100,000 in it, her discount brokerage firm now charges only $6.95 per trade, instead of the minimum fee of $29.95 for smaller accounts.

A buy or a sell constitutes one trade. So if Carla sells one hundred shares of Imperial Oil and buys one hundred shares of Bell Canada Enterprises (BCE), she has made two trades—one sell and one buy—at $6.95 each.

Carla averages about twenty-four trades a year and estimates that she spends two to four hours a week researching and managing her portfolio.

The market has been so full of gyrations in the past five years that few individual investors can boast Carla's record. What's more, very few mutual funds have been able to beat their respective benchmark indices. To assess their performance, mutual funds are compared to a benchmark index. A mutual fund holding mostly big Canadian companies would be compared to the S&P/TSX 60 Index (an index of Canada's largest sixty companies), while a mutual fund holding mostly big US companies could be compared to either the Dow Jones Industrial Average (thirty of America's largest companies) or the broader S&P 500 (five hundred of the largest publicly traded American companies).

I know what you're thinking. You're looking at Carla's 5.3 per cent average annual ten-year return and thinking the number is pathetic. "This is not much more than she would have received if she'd simply put the money into a GIC and rolled it over," you're probably saying, "all at zero risk and little time spent." And you're right! Remember what I said in the previous chapter about a guaranteed return being something to love? These numbers just go to show why.

Carla is one kind of investor, an active one. She buys and sells, researches companies, and attempts to get in and out at the best possible price. But if someone like Carla, who has intimate knowledge of a sector in the economy and devotes plenty of time to study and research, can only generate little more than 5 per cent return over the past ten years, what hope does the average investor have?

Actually, plenty of hope! Let me introduce you to two investors with a very different investment style.

$

Case Study: Juan, 41, and Marie, 43

Juan and Marie are married with two preteen children. They have $80,000 in his RRSP and $38,000 in hers. Juan manages a food distribution warehouse, is devoted to his girls, and has a passion for growing vegetables from seed. Marie, who works at a radio station, is a continuing education junkie, taking three or four classes annually in everything from Photoshop to culinary arts.

Juan and Marie describe themselves as being rather lazy financially, especially when it comes to their RRSPs. But I think they simply have a good understanding of who they are as investors. Between work, their daughters' sports practices and competitions, hours in the greenhouse and garden, and courses at the nearby community college, they pack a lot of living into each day.

They knew from the beginning of their investing lives that they weren't going to have the time—or the desire—to manage or monitor anything fancy. They had read about the high fees for mutual funds and were put off by them, and they didn't have enough money to work with a wealth manager.

.... **$** ....

I'm going to give myself a little pat on the back. Juan and Marie read a series of columns I wrote back in 1999 on passive investing. Passive investing, which is the heart of the investment strategy in this book, involves purchasing those low-fee ETFs I mentioned in the previous chapters—units of an equity or bond index (like the S&P 500 or the DEX Long Bond Index), rather than individual stocks or mutual funds. The key to passive investing is to decide on an asset allocation and have the discipline to stick to it by rebalancing occasionally, adding new contributions, and reinvesting dividends. Juan and Marie decided this was the perfect approach for them. And I believe it's perfect for most of you too!

Here's the asset allocation Juan and Marie chose for both their RRSPs:

Cash	10 per cent	1 one-year GIC
Bonds	50 per cent	1 bond ETF
Equities	40 per cent	1 Canadian equity ETF

Juan and Marie's equity ETF holds the same stocks that are in the Canadian S&P/TSX Composite Index (roughly two hundred stocks). More on this later.

Here's how their average annual rate of return stacks up against Carla's and the broader US and Canadian markets:

	JUAN AND MARIE'S RRSPS (PER CENT)	CARLA'S RRSP (PER CENT)	S&P/TSX COMPOSITE INDEX TOTAL RETURN (CANADIAN) (PER CENT)	S&P 500 INDEX TOTAL RETURN (US) (PER CENT)
1 year	11	19	20.9	18.4
3 years	4.2	0.3	0.2	1.4
5 years	6.8	4.2	5.7	0
10 years	7.9	5.3	8	−1.8

Over the past ten years, Juan and Marie have enjoyed a better return than Carla, even though they have 50 per cent of their RRSP in cash and bonds. They've also handily beaten the market over most time periods as well. And better still, they've spent far less time doing it.

Those unloved investments, cash and bonds, have provided ballast in choppy stock market seas. I know I'm harping on this, but remember what I said about the delights of a guaranteed return! With 60 per cent of their savings in these two baskets, Juan and Marie are protected when the stock market takes a powder, as it has done twice in the last ten years. With only 40 per cent of their money in equities, they are much less exposed to the vagaries of the market.

But the other reason for Juan and Marie's healthier returns is that they're good at housekeeping. Once a year they take a look at their asset allocation, or how they've spread their eggs. If it has moved appreciably from the 10/50/40 split they settled on long ago, they move it back by selling something or using new contributions to rebalance. That's portfolio housekeeping.

Juan and Marie have shown great discipline in sticking to their asset allocation. New money is invested in order to keep their eggs spread according to that initial decision. They leave their monthly contributions in cash in their RRSPs, and they invest and rebalance annually to keep their trading fees low. And they spend far less time at it than the average of thirty minutes a month I promised at the beginning of the book.

The stock market changes and so do interest rates. Juan loses a little more hair up top and gains a little more elsewhere. Marie switches up her continuing education hobby, and their girls grow like Juan's coddled veggies when he sets them out in May. But their asset allocation doesn't change. It might if something dramatic happens in their lives, such as a job loss. Barring that, their AA will stay the same until they get closer to retirement, but they are twenty years from that point.

When the markets were booming, between 2005 and early 2007, Juan and Marie put most of their new RRSP contributions in bonds and cash, keeping to the same 10/50/40 ratios. Come mid-2008, when all hell broke loose over the subprime mortgage mess, the market crashed and their equity ETF portion did as well, sinking to 28 per cent. To compensate, they simply rearranged their new money eggs and contributed more to the equity portion of their portfolios to bring it back to around 40 per cent.

In mid-2009, when the market bottomed out, the equity portion dropped again. So Juan and Marie once again used their new RRSP contributions to bring it back to 40 per cent. In other words, as everyone else was stampeding away from the stock market, Juan and Marie were waltzing toward it—but not because they had a crystal ball and predicted the market would boom, as it did the next year. They just followed their plan of staying with their asset allocation mix. They didn't get carried away with rebalancing, however. The key to rebalancing is getting your portfolio close to its original asset allocation without generating unnecessary trading fees. Being off a bit over time isn't really an issue.

In 2010 most of Juan and Marie's new contributions went into the bond and cash basket to maintain that 10/50/40 allocation because the stock market had a much better year. It's all about sticking with the program. Portfolio housekeeping, or rebalancing, drives a healthy return and keeps risk at bay. It's a simple and incredibly effective way of making investment decisions, and I've found it becomes almost second nature over time. It also reduces the incidence of those fatal mistakes that investors (including the pros) make: second guessing, buying too much of one thing and not enough of another, making wrong decisions about when to buy and sell, and getting panicked or carried away by the noise of the market.

If it were an easy thing to know when to get in and out of the market, you wouldn't need this book. In fact, if you can predict bull and bear markets with accuracy, know in advance when a scandal will devastate a company, or foresee when war will interrupt the flow of oil, you don't need *any* book!

Lower That Risk!

Of course, Juan and Marie's RRSP will never have the potential to increase as much as Carla's during a stock market boom because they have a lower percentage of their money in equities. However, they also won't lose as much when the market goes down, in part because of the return generated by the cash and bonds. Put another way, their portfolio is far less risky than Carla's. That means they are much less likely to lose money at any given time, and they are also less likely to grab the brass ring. But that's no problem. Few investors are able to grab that brass ring even when it is dangling right in front of them. They don't get into a stock just before it's ready to soar and they don't get out before it crashes. The investor directive to buy low and sell high is actually very hard to do.

Juan and Marie's asset allocation works for them, but yours may be different. An asset allocation is an individual thing, and as I showed in chapter 8, it depends on your time frame, situation, and temperament. It also depends on which investment box you are talking about.

Here are some examples of possible asset allocations for different accounts and different stages of life:

- TFSA (for a young couple saving to buy a house in two to three years): 100 per cent cash (GICs)
- RESP (for kids under thirteen): 50 per cent bonds, 50 per cent equities
- RESP (for kids over thirteen): 50 per cent cash (GICs), 50 per cent bonds
- RRSP (for someone five years from retirement): 15 per cent cash, 50 per cent bonds, 35 per cent equities
- RRSP (for someone fifteen years or more from retirement): 10 per cent cash, 40 per cent bonds, 50 per cent equities

You can pick one of the AAs above or create your own, something you'll learn more about as this book progresses. But don't worry—there is no right or wrong way of doing this. The key is to spread your money among the three main asset classes, then rebalance and reinvest occasionally. This is far more important than worrying about whether you should have 40 per cent invested in bonds or 30 per cent.

But how do you determine what mix is right for you? And how do you maintain that mix once you've got it in place? All you really need to do is follow these five simple steps:

1. Pick your investment boxes and be clear about your time frame.
2. Select an asset allocation that is appropriate to your time frame and tolerance for risk. For example, if you're five years from retirement, you'll probably want more money in bonds and less in stocks; if you're twenty years from retirement, you'll probably want it the other way around.
3. Review your investment mix once or twice a year.
4. Rebalance and reinvest when your asset allocation gets "out of whack"—that is, drifts too far from your original percentages.
5. Keep your portfolio simple and don't fret about the market "noise."

You now have the makings of a portfolio plan.

Spread Your Eggs Further?

I just know what some of you are thinking: if spreading your eggs around is good, then why not spread them around even further within the three major asset classes—cash, bonds and equities? This is called diversification.

The research on this is clear: *some* diversification improves your return and reduces risk. But too much can actually harm your portfolio's performance over time. Too much diversification also violates the KISS principle—a serious infraction in my books. Keep your portfolio simple and you'll be able to keep on top of it and do the maintenance, which is so critical to the long-term growth of your portfolio.

I'd further advise you not to worry about diversifying in the cash and fixed income baskets unless you have a substantial amount in each area—say, $50,000 or more. Just stick with short-term GICs and roll them over as they come due. (Of course, if we once again find ourselves in the midst of double-digit inflation—à la 1982—by all means go for the longest, highest-paying term you can find and laugh all the way to the bank.) I recommend the same approach with bonds. You could diversify and buy different bonds all over the world maturing at different times, but you don't need to. Just stick with a single broad-based bond investment and keep the term short to medium. The exception to this rule would be those who have a large amount invested in bonds—say, $100,000 or more—and are investing for income. In this case, a group, or ladder, of short-, medium-, and long-term bonds will generate the highest return. But you don't need to buy lots of different bonds to do this. You can "ladder" your bond portfolio over time with a handful of ETFs.

In the Take Action section, I'll give you a number of easy-to-follow sample portfolios to choose from and you'll see bond investing in action. Remember to keep it simple, smarty!

So what about equities? Believe it or not, you don't need to spread those eggs too far afield either. In fact, you'll be a lot better off if you don't spread them too far. Over the years, I've heard numerous strident investment assertions. Among them: "You need to be invested in Japan!" "You've got to have money in the Six Tigers." "Latin America is the next big juggernaut!" "The developing world needs commodities—don't leave that sector out!" "Forget old economy, get into technology!" Invariably those sectors or countries tanked—some for lengthy periods—within a year.

Research shows very clearly that you don't need to fling your equity investments far and wide to be well diversified. Indeed, too much diversification can actually decrease your return and increase your risk. If you have too much crammed into your investment portfolio—whether it's an RRSP, an RESP, or a non-registered account—you won't be able to pay attention to it all. You are also more likely to be confused about what you hold, and therefore less able to make decisions about how to manage those holdings.

Though I am not a fan of mutual funds, they are very popular with Canadians, and I recognize that investor behaviour isn't going to change any time soon. So if you are going to invest in mutual funds for the equity part of your portfolio, I recommend you limit yourself to no more than two or three of them. And if you follow my advice and invest in exchange-traded funds for equities, one broadly based US ETF and one broadly based Canadian ETF will do you quite nicely.

"But wait!" you say. "What about China and India and Australia? What if Europe pulls itself out of the economic toilet? Shouldn't I own something that invests in those places?"

If you do as I suggest, you will in effect have investments in all those places. Big companies do business all over the world. So if you buy broadly based US and Canadian ETFs, your money will be working for you in far-flung regions because today's large and even medium companies are increasingly global.

With some cash, some bonds, and a couple of equity products, you will have a clean, simple, inexpensive, and well-diversified

portfolio. Just look what happens when you spread your eggs as I
am recommending:

	PORTFOLIO 1 (PER CENT)	PORTFOLIO 2 (PER CENT)
TSX/S&P Composite Index	100	25
S&P 500 Index	0	25
Canadian Bonds	0	40
Five-year GICs	0	10
Return 1991–2011	8.0	7.3

If you had a single investment, either a mutual fund or an
exchange-traded fund that closely matched the Canadian S&P/
TSX Composite Index (portfolio #1), your twenty-year return
would have been 8 per cent after dividends were included. Spreading your eggs around just a bit—into bonds, some cash, and the
US market—would have resulted in an annual return of 7.3 per
cent over twenty years.

There's hardly any difference, right? Wrong. The undiversified
first portfolio is much riskier than the diversified second portfolio.
That means that at any given time over the past twenty years, you
would have been far more likely to lose money with the first portfolio than with the more conservative and safer second portfolio.

The lessons of this chapter are:

1. Choose an asset allocation from the three asset classes—cash,
   fixed income, and equities.
2. Pick a small number of investment products to fit that allocation.
3. Stick to that asset allocation over time by rebalancing or adding new money.

By doing these three things, you will build a solid investment
foundation with a low-risk, low-fee, low-maintenance portfolio
that actually produces a better return than the riskier portfolio.
Isn't that what everyone wants?

CHAPTER 11

Fry Those Fees

You now have a working knowledge of asset allocation and understand how critical it is to your investment return. Just by choosing an asset allocation, sticking with it over time, and rebalancing periodically to get back to the percentages you originally chose, you will help your portfolio grow. But there is one other major obstacle in the way of maximizing your investment returns and minimizing your losses: fees.

In all their many forms, fees are a growth killer. Good investments turn into bad ones when big fees are attached to buying, selling, and holding. DIYers who invest in stocks are warned not to run up trading fees, especially for small trades, because it eats into return. But too few investors realize how debilitating annual mutual fund fees, called management expense ratios (MERs), are to their long-term returns.

$

Case Study: Sonja, 56

As she nears retirement, Sonja is looking forward to many years of focusing on her new boyfriend, three children, and two grandchildren. A single mother, she has never been part of a company pension plan. Her job as a public relations contractor in the entertainment industry paid modestly, but she has been diligently putting aside money since her mid-twenties.

By the time Sonja was forty-one, in 1996, she had about $60,000 in her RRSP, most of it in GICs, Canada Savings Bonds, and a Government of Canada bond. When the bonds matured, she simply rolled them over into new ones. It was a simple investment program that her father had helped put into place, and she stuck with it while her children were young.

When her father died that year and left her $40,000, Sonja consulted an adviser at the bank where she had her RRSP account. He strongly recommended she put her inheritance, plus the $60,000 she already had in her RRSP, into equity mutual funds in order to reach her goal of retiring at age sixty, in 2015. A group of professionally managed equity mutual funds investing in the stock market, he insisted, would really boost her RRSP growth. Sonja could expect an 8 per cent average annual rate of return, he assured her; in those days that was considered a pretty conservative forecast. Using that figure, he projected that her RRSP would be worth about $320,000 by the time she was ready to retire. That sold Sonja.

Sonja reinvested her money as her adviser suggested. Over the ensuing fifteen years, she contributed nothing more to her RRSPs and instead concentrated on paying off her mortgage. Her goal was to be debt-free with that $320,000 to generate income when she retired at sixty.

But when she reached fifty-six in 2011, Sonja's RRSP was worth just over $180,000—a long way from $330,000. The bursting of the tech bubble, the market sag after 9/11, and the financial crisis of 2008 had flattened her funds. She had managed an average return over the previous fifteen years of 4 per cent—half what her adviser forecast. Her bottom line was improving by 2011, but not nearly enough, so Sonja was forced to change her plans and work full-time until sixty-five. She was lucky that she had a steady income and working an additional five years was possible.

Sonja held six mutual funds in her RRSP. What she hadn't realized was how much of a headwind the MERs had created for growth in her mutual funds. She'd just assumed that the stock market roller coaster and the dreadful world economy had conspired to reduce her hoped-for annual return. She didn't know how much she had spent on fees to get that 4 per cent return over fifteen years. Brace yourselves—here it is:

more than $50,000![*]

That's right, Sonja had spent around $300 every single month for fifteen years after she reinvested her RRSP funds. That $80,000 gain in her RRSP—nowhere close to the $320,000 she'd been expecting—had cost her $54,000 to achieve.

If Sonja had instead added her $40,000 inheritance to her existing RRSP in 1996 and purchased more bonds, she would have had nearly $237,000 in 2011 (based on the actual 5.9 per cent average annual compounded return for that period). I'm really not making a pitch to eschew the stock market, but I want you to know that with mutual funds, you frequently don't get what you pay for.

I have often wondered why those who rigorously scrutinize the cost of cellphone packages, purchase generic painkillers over their brand-name cousins, and comparison shop like crazy in the grocery store never apply the same focus to their investments. Over the years, I have asked hundreds of investors one or more of the following questions:

- What do your mutual funds cost you?
- How expensive is your portfolio?

---

[*] According to the fee calculator at getsmarteraboutmoney.ca.

- What are you paying in fees?
- What are your investing costs?

Most of the time, I get nothing but blank looks, as if I had asked about the cost of a smile or the price of fresh air. Some people actually believe they aren't paying any fees for their mutual funds. I have a friend whose fund manager is a long-time pal. She always tells me that her friend/adviser invests her money in mutual funds as a favour, free of charge, gratis. I have tried to convince her that he gets paid by the fund companies from fees embedded in her funds, but she doesn't want to hear it—she prefers to believe in the fairy tale.

Are You Getting What You Pay For?

David Chilton, the author of the two Wealthy Barber bestsellers, talks about this puzzling ambivalence toward fees in his entertaining seminars. He points out that to most people, a 2.5 per cent fee doesn't sound like much. And it's true. If I tell you that an item costs $100 and fees will add another 2.5 per cent, or a mere $2.50, you are likely to shrug. In an age when sales taxes add 13 to 15 per cent to the cost of so many goods and services, 2.5 per cent seems like a real bargain.

There are always nods of agreement in the audience over Chilton's comments. Then he neatly flips things around by pointing out that if a mutual fund produces an 8 per cent return before fees in a given year, that 2.5 per cent fee portion eats up a staggering 31 per cent of that gain. Not only that, but you pay those fees year in and year out, for as long as you hold the fund. What's more, the fund always gets paid before you do. If the fee is 2.5 per cent and the fund makes only 2.5 per cent in one year, your gain is zero.

The industry argues that the MER covers the cost of ongoing professional management from the portfolio team and advice from the fund salesperson. Part of that MER is something called a trailer fee. Between 0.25 and 0.75 per cent goes annually, in some combination, to the salesperson or firm that sold you the fund to pay for advice and service. If the fund manager is adding value and the salesperson is providing service, then of course you should expect to pay. But therein lies the rub. Adding value should mean that the pros are getting you a better return than the fund's benchmark index. And service should mean more than contact during the initial sale and a phone call now and then to sell you more product.

Paying those annual fees is not so hard to take in a booming stock market, when returns of 12 to 20 per cent are common for both mutual fund and stock portfolios. But in a flat, or even just average, market, anywhere from 25 to 40 per cent of your return will be gobbled up by fees. The small bite turns into an investor-eating tiger chomp when the market is in decline, and the fees you pay annually turn losses into bigger losses.

The lesson is this:

- Fees = smaller profits
- Fees = bigger losses
- Fees = unachievable investment goals

$

Case Study: Suzette, 29, assistant producer

I worked with Suzette on my television show *Maxed Out* in 2006. She had started investing two years earlier and was very proud of herself for contributing to her RRSP every month. Her father had given her a $1,000 gift to kick-start her portfolio, and on the recommendation of an adviser with one of the large firms, she had been investing $200 monthly in four funds—$50 in each. She'd just come back from a meeting with her adviser and was bubbling over with good cheer; he'd told her that her portfolio was performing "extremely well."

I hesitated for a moment, but my curiosity got the better of me. "Do you have a statement?" I ventured. She did. A little quick math showed that the total contributions from Suzette and her father amounted to $5,800 over two years. The current bottom line was $5,900, basically what she would have earned if the money had been in a high-interest savings account. Not much of a gain in a hot market.

$

My quick once-over of Suzette's mutual funds quickly revealed why she had made such a small gain. The funds came with a 5 per cent front-end load fee that was applied to every contribution. The average MER for the funds was 2.85 per cent, and three of her four funds were subpar—performing in the bottom half of their categories or peer groups. The grand total of fees paid to the fund company and the adviser over the two years was $536. Suzette didn't know that she was paying fees in the form of high MERs and a front-end load with every purchase. The fees didn't appear anywhere on her statement, and it wasn't part of the discussion when the adviser set her up with her portfolio.

I took a chance and explained it all to Suzette. But perhaps that was a mistake, because she was royally ticked off at the time and the relationship has since cooled. No good deed goes unpunished.

When you don't know the fees, let alone what performance those fees have been purchasing, you are investing blindfolded.

I've been criticizing the lack of clarity on investment statements for years. In 2010, DALBAR, a US-based investment research firm, surveyed investors to find out what they most wanted to see on their statements. Not surprisingly, the top two items were rate of return and total fees charged. DALBAR's research discovered that only 23 per cent of Canadian mutual fund companies displayed the rate of return on their statements.

Worse, only 6 per cent of brokerage statements (such as you'd get at a full-service or discount brokerage) carried that information.

You've probably figured out by now that I'm not a big fan of mutual funds, and fees are one of the primary reasons. The problem is not just that they are far, far too high—double and sometimes triple those charged by comparable US mutual fund companies—but that they're not transparent. Do you ever see the management fees spelled out on your investment statement? Does your adviser point out, without being asked, what fees you will be paying? Does he or she explain to whom that money is going? Are low-priced alternatives such as exchange-traded funds or even reduced-fee mutual funds offered for consideration? Usually not.

Most of you may not even realize there are low-fee versions of many mutual funds—called F Series funds. These are generally designed for advisers who charge their clients a flat percentage to manage their accounts or work on a fee-for-service basis. There are also cheaper versions of many funds aimed at the DIYer, and these have a lower MER. RBC, for example, pioneered low-fee Series D funds for those investing without an adviser. But if you don't know what you're looking for, you may have trouble finding them.

Years ago, when I first started an RESP for my two daughters, I purchased three mutual funds for the account, including one focused on Europe. Only after I had been purchasing units of these three funds for a couple of years did I discover that the European fund, with its management expense ratio of 2.97 per cent, existed in a low-MER version of 2.27 per cent. When I called my discount brokerage to ask about this, I was told, "Oh yes, the low-fee fund is available, but you have to ask for it and it isn't available for online trades."

Great. If I don't know it exists, what would prompt me to ask for it?

Today, there are many more low-fee mutual funds available, but if you are trading online, you may end up with the higher-fee fund unless you know what to look for.

And More Fees

There are other fees to be concerned about with mutual funds as well. There may be sales commissions, also called load fees. Some—front-end load fees—you pay when purchasing a fund. Others—back-end load fees, or more commonly, deferred sales charges (DSCs)—you pay if you sell within a certain time period. Front-end load fees are typically as much as 5 per cent of your purchase price. So if you are investing $10,000, you will lose $500 right off the top. As a result, only $9,500 is working for you. And you'd be amazed what a difference that makes. Take a gander:

	FRONT-END LOAD (5 PER CENT) MUTUAL FUND	NO-LOAD MUTUAL FUND
Initial Investment	$ 9,500 ($500 to fee)	$10,000
Monthly Investment	$ 237.50 ($12.50 to fee)	$ 250
Rate of Return Annually (per cent)	5	5
Total After 15 Years	$83,561	$87,959

No, you're not seeing things. You will have lost almost $4,500 in fifteen years simply because of the front-end load fee.

"I'll get around that fee!" you say. "I'll buy deferred sales charge mutual funds. If I hold them until the DSC declines to zero [that can be anywhere from three to six years], I'll pay no fees!"

Good thinking. Or is it? DSC fees can be as big a problem as their front-end load cousins. Let's say you have a really howling hound of a fund, or even one that's just a bit of a pooch. You're tired of poor returns, so you decide to sell. But wait a minute! You've owned that fund for only a couple of years, which means that you will be charged a fee to get out. What do you do?

Investor behaviour tells us that while most of us ignore, or are unaware of, the fees when we're buying and holding funds, we'll often hang on to underperformers just to avoid the exit charge. That means DSC funds cost us money in the form of opportunity cost. You feel locked in because of that fee. If your fund has a six-year holding period and you sell at the midpoint, it will cost you 3 to 4 per cent in sales fees. Typically, you hang on to avoid the fee. But if the fund is a poor performer, you are losing money not only because of its subpar returns but also because you could put that money to work elsewhere. That's opportunity cost. The longer you hold a bad investment, the higher your opportunity cost.

Investment fees are like hurdles you have to clear to get to the finish line. The higher they are, the longer it will take you to reach your goals and the more likely you are to fall. A mutual fund company has to strap on its track shoes and leap the fee hurdle before you start making money. If the hurdle is one foot high, or the fee is 1 per cent, then it isn't too hard to clear. But if the hurdle is two or three feet, or 2 or 3 per cent, the fund company has to jump that much higher—in other words, make that gain first—before *you* start making money. If you have DSC funds and don't plan to sell until the fee has expired, it still sits there, like a hurdle on the sidelines, waiting to be flung into your path.

And one more thing about those DSC fees: research shows that it's a much better strategy to invest on a regular basis, monthly or quarterly, than to invest irregular lump sums. That's that theory of dollar cost averaging I mentioned earlier. But if you contribute monthly to an array of DSC mutual funds, every new dollar brings with it a new fee schedule. The contribution you made last month will carry that DSC charge three to six years into the future.

Of course, just as there's no such thing as a free lunch, there's no such thing as no-fee investing either. All investments have some sort of cost. Even if you purchase stocks or exchange-traded funds, you will still pay a trading fee ranging from $6.95 to nearly $30 per trade. The standard minimum trading fee at the major banks' discount brokerages used to be close to $30 for almost every retail investor except the hyperactive traders. Happily that has changed. Now if you have $50,000 to $100,000 in your investment account or in business with your bank (such as a mortgage or a line of credit), the cost per trade has dropped to between $6.95 and $9.95. Fortunately, this change makes it more practical for everyday folk to buy my favourite investment product—exchange-traded funds—on a regular basis without getting hit by a big trading fee. Although ETFs do have management fees, they are minuscule compared to those of mutual funds.

The bottom line is this: you can't predict the stock market, let alone control it. And if your crystal ball is as cloudy as mine, you have no idea when or where the ups and downs of the economy will come. Nor do you have any say in what mutual fund managers do with your money. Worse still, you don't have a vote if mutual fund A suddenly is absorbed by mutual fund B and you're left with a different investment than the one you started with. (This happens all the time with mutual funds.) But you can control fees. Here's how:

- Know what fees you're paying. Ask questions! What is the MER? Are there front-end load fees or deferred sales charge fees?
- Negotiate both load and MER fees if you are using an adviser.
- Ask for low-fee versions of mutual funds at your discount brokerage if you are a DIYer.

It doesn't take much to do this, but over time you will put thousands of dollars back in your pocket.

Of course, one of the best ways to avoid noxiously high fees is not to invest in mutual funds in the first place. Instead, count on yourself. Page on over to the next section to learn how to put together (on your own or with an adviser) your own simple, low-fee, low-stress portfolio.

PART 4

TAKE
ACTION

CHAPTER 12

Meet the Easy Chair

The Easy Chair isn't a comfy spot to sit—it's a comfy place to invest, a safe location to park your investment butt. This little portfolio is inexpensive and perfect for both DIYers and those with investment advisers. It is balanced, flexible, low maintenance, and has a built-in discipline that helps avoid the money-losing decisions that plague so many investors.

In short, the Easy Chair is a portfolio for virtually everyone. It fits most people and can be adjusted to the majority of situations. Whether you're retired or newly pregnant, at the peak of earning or near the end of your working life, the Easy Chair can be tailored to fit your needs.

Unfortunately, few commission-based advisers recommend anything like the Easy Chair. Its management costs are extremely low and there are no trailer fees, deferred sales charges, or front-end commissions. In other words, no go-betweens get paid for selling the components of the Easy Chair—even though many, if not most, admit when pressed that it's a perfect little portfolio.

Here's how I met the Easy Chair and invited it into my living room.

Back in the mid-1990s, David and I started writing a new column for the *Toronto Star* called "Choice Portfolios." The concept was to give a group of experts an imaginary $50,000 to invest and then follow the portfolios weekly, reporting on their performance and the experts' investment decisions. To be frank, the idea was a completely selfish one. Although we had been writing about business and the economy for years at that point, I was increasingly interested in the stock market and wanted to understand more of its wily ways. How better to accomplish that, I thought, than to be paid as we learned?

At first, I thought that given a platform like the *Toronto Star*, the largest newspaper in the country, experts would be clamouring for a spot. Not hardly! In fact, not at all. It was almost impossible to find economic gurus, fund managers, analysts, brokers, or other advisers willing to put themselves on the line by having their investment choices scrutinized every week. Ultimately, I came to understand their reluctance. Participating in a newspaper column, with your investment choices, good and bad, laid out for all to see, is a daunting prospect. It is particularly unnerving because short-term comparisons—we'd be following the portfolios for just a year—can be very misleading. The way the stock market moves, today's flavour of the month is tomorrow's has-been.

Eventually, we convinced four brave souls from the finance world to invest and manage these imaginary portfolios. But we wanted five because a larger number would provide more journalistic variety and allow us to talk about lots of different issues, from a range of perspectives, over the course of the year. Finally, one analyst suggested we contact an academic by the name of Eric Kirzner, an internationally known economist and a professor of finance at the esteemed Rotman School of Management at the University of Toronto. Kirzner sat on a number of prominent corporate boards, served as an adviser to several large pension funds, and acted as an expert witness in numerous high-profile corporate lawsuits.

Kirzner seemed a little too good to be true. He had no need of media face time and nothing to sell, so we weren't sure why he'd want to take part. But when we approached him, it turned out that he had an idea he wanted to explore, and "Choice Portfolios" offered the perfect platform to do that. He intended to create what he called a passive portfolio.

I'd never heard the word *passive* applied to the investing world. In fact, the term *passive investing* seemed an oxymoron, like *military intelligence* or *jumbo shrimp*. The very word *passive*—as in, do nothing—didn't seem to mesh with the idea of making money.

Kirzner agreed that passive investing sounded like a contradiction in terms. But he believed this approach would allow him to create a portfolio that would generate a reasonable return, yet allow people to sleep at night. "You don't face gambler's ruin with it," he explained. "You can't pick the wrong stock or fund because you're not picking a single one." He also wanted the portfolio to be comprehensible to those without a lot of investment experience.

And so, in April 1997, Eric Kirzner's portfolio—which we dubbed the Easy Chair—joined four others:

1. The Big Blue—100 per cent Canadian stocks
2. Stars and Stripes—100 per cent US stocks
3. The Peach—100 per cent junior mining stocks
4. Uncle Sam—a portfolio based on technical analysis

> Technical analysts use a host of variables, including trading volume, market trends, and short- and long-term price movements, to determine what to trade and when. The technique involves using charts, statistics, and signals (like stochastic oscillators, if you want to impress people) to guide investment decisions.

Kirzner believed that the ideal portfolio for most investors would begin with an asset allocation based on safety, income, and growth. Here's how he incorporated these three elements into the original Easy Chair:

- Safety—20 per cent cash
- Income—30 per cent bonds
- Growth—35 per cent Canadian equities
- Growth—15 per cent US equities

None of the other portfolios included cash or bonds, or indeed had an asset allocation other than 100 per cent equities. But where Kirzner really differed from his "Choice Portfolio" colleagues was in how he invested in equities, or the stock part of the portfolio. He didn't actually buy any individual stocks or even any mutual funds. He simply invested in pieces of the two major Canadian and US stock market indices—just as if he had purchased slices of two different pies.

The Canadian equity investment came in the form of a pioneering product called TIPS 35, which mirrored the performance of the TSE 35 Index, a now defunct index composed of Canada's thirty-five largest companies. Created in 1981, TIPS 35 was actually the groundbreaker in the development of what were originally called index products and are now known as exchange-traded funds (I'll explain them fully in chapter 14). It wasn't a mutual fund—there was no buying and selling, no shorting, and no optioning within it. The product simply held the same thirty-five large Canadian companies that existed in the TSE 35 Index.

When you bought units of TIPS 35, you owned a slice of each of those thirty-five companies, in the same proportion as their value in the index. If the aggregate of the thirty-five companies went up in value—that is, the index rose—your slice of them went up accordingly, and when the Canadian market declined, the value of TIPS did the same. TIPS also paid dividends to unit-holders, again in the same proportion as companies in the index did.

Investing in an index is the essence of passive investing. These products aren't like mutual funds, where a manager is always buying and selling in an attempt to beat the market. The job of these index funds or ETFs (then and now) is to mirror the performance of an index. That's it. TIPS 35 was a pioneer in what has become a global revolution in investing. But in 1997, when Eric Kirzner selected it for the Easy Chair portfolio, hardly anyone knew anything about index funds.

For the US end of things, Kirzner purchased a similar product

that tracked the S&P 500 Index. It was called Standard & Poor's
Depositary Receipts (SPDR)—a long and fancy name for a basket
that replicates, or copies, the five hundred stocks in the index.
SPDR was (and still is) listed on the New York Stock Exchange
(NYSE) under the ticker symbol SPY.

The attraction of these two equity index products was low
fees—just half a per cent annually, which was much lower than
the average mutual fund fee at the time of 2.65 per cent. Units
traded like any stock, and the owners received their share of
whatever dividends were paid out by the companies in the index.

Here's how the four investments in the Easy Chair looked:

20% cash	$10,000	Beutel Goodman Money Market Fund
30% bonds	$15,000	7 per cent Gov't. of Canada bond (maturing in 2006)
35% Canadian equities	$17,500	TIPS 35 (TSE 35 Index)
15% US equities	$7,500	SPDR (S&P 500 Index)

It cost Kirzner $57.90 in trading fees to purchase the two
index products. There was no purchase fee on the money market
fund, and the fee for the bond was blended into the purchase price.

By backdating the portfolio historically for thirty years,
Kirzner estimated that it would average a return of around 8
per cent annually (after dividends and interest income were reinvested). "People tell me they're surprised I've chosen such a conservative mix," he said a month after the Easy Chair debuted. "But
it's only viewed as conservative because the markets have been
so strong. I'd say if you went back a few years, people would have
said it's kind of aggressive."

In fact, the word *surprised* doesn't begin to describe the reac-
tion to the Easy Chair. There was derision, scoffing, and outright
pity. Yes, pity. It seemed poor Eric, the woolly-headed academic, didn't have a clue about investing and so defaulted to this

nonentity of a portfolio. "That thing will never beat the market," people sneered. "They miss the point," Kirzner replied complacently. "I don't want to beat the market. I want the Easy Chair to achieve the same returns as the market itself." One of the other "Choice Portfolio" experts said bluntly, "He's going to get killed. I feel sorry for him." And the man was right . . . at first.

In 1997, stock markets worldwide were in the middle of a long bull run. Since 1991, stocks globally had been shooting up almost without pause. Returns of 15 to 18 per cent and more were common in the late 1990s for mutual funds and stock portfolios alike. Even though these numbers far outstripped historical returns, they came to be accepted as the new normal, particularly by the neophyte investors and advisers who had flooded into the market as the bull kept running.

After ten months, we had written about the Easy Chair only four times because nothing much happened with it. Kirzner did no trading, added no new investments—nothing. It was all quite boring from a journalism perspective. The Easy Chair produced a good return that year, but its growth was pitiful compared to the other portfolios.

> Many different definitions for "return" are bandied about
> in the investment industry. Average annual compounded
> return includes each year's gain—plus interest or dividend
> payments—averaged over a given time period.

Throughout most of 1997 and the first half of 1998, the Easy Chair grew at a rate of 13 to 14 per cent. Each time we asked him about the gains, Kirzner said more or less the same thing: "It's getting a bit ahead of itself." At the end of the one-year period, April 1998, here's how the five portfolios looked:

1. Uncle Sam—   up over 200 per cent to $151,500
2. Stars and Stripes—   up 27 per cent to $63,500

3. The Big Blue—	up 19 per cent to $59,500
4. The Easy Chair—	up 13.5 per cent to $56,750
5. The Peach—	down 8 per cent to $46,810

The eye-popping Uncle Sam portfolio was a fun ride. Colman O'Brien, then a technical analyst and now a private wealth manager, used a variety of trading tricks, watching market signals (triple tops, double flags, oscillators) to tell him when to pounce. He often held only a single stock in his portfolio, and sometimes just for a few days. I understood what he was doing barely half the time. The high wire that O'Brien walked was not for the faint of heart, but he did come out on top.

Kirzner looked at the results and said, "Good for them." Then he did nothing. Actually, that's not quite true. Remember chapter 10, where I talked about portfolio housekeeping? Juan and Marie had picked an asset allocation, and every now and then they rebalanced their portfolio to get it back to the original percentages. Eric Kirzner did the same thing. The Easy Chair was rebalanced in 1998, for example, when the equity portion of the portfolio jumped from 50 to 62 per cent. He sold a bit of the US index product and a bit of the Canadian index product, added cash that had accumulated from the bond and from dividends, then put it all in the money market fund, which had fallen from 20 per cent to 13. If Kirzner had been making contributions regularly, he would have used the new cash to rebalance and likely would not have had to sell anything. Apart from that minimal amount of housekeeping, Kirzner just left his portfolio alone.

The Little Portfolio That Could

We moved on to new portfolios for a second season of the column. Just as we were wrapping them up in mid-1999, we paid another visit to the Easy Chair because we were curious about how the passive-investing approach would work over time. The markets were getting as hot as beach sand in August. Technology was on a tear. You couldn't pick up a newspaper or magazine without reading about the wonders of the wireless world and how it was going to reshape the global economy. No one would shop in bricks-and-mortar stores anymore—it would all be cybermalls. The virtual world was exploding.

The "old economy," as it was disdainfully called, had sagged. Financials, consumer stocks, and utilities were yesterday's news. No one wanted a stock that paid a reliable dividend and grew by only 10 or 12 per cent a year. "New economy" stocks like Nortel Networks, Cisco Systems, JDS Uniphase, Enron, and Worldcom were the future. They paid little or no dividends but boasted monstrous growth—30, 40, and 50 per cent annually. The markets of the Far East, the Middle East, and South America—all growing like joyous weeds—also tantalized.

The technology-laden NASDAQ soared 35 per cent in 1999. The Easy Chair gained almost 18 per cent that year. "Too much," said Kirzner, shaking his head. "This growth is an aberration. I still stick to my prediction that 8 per cent or so will be the annual average over time." He felt that the equity markets were overheated and would return to lower historical growth rates over the long run.

There was the briefest of pullbacks in late 1999, as the world braced for the impact of Y2K. But when January 1, 2000, dawned like any other year and nothing happened, the tech tear resumed as if it would never end.

But of course, it did.

By late 2000, high-tech stock carcasses littered the planet. The NASDAQ plummeted 78 per cent after hitting its peak on March 10, 2000. Many mutual funds were flattened. Even so, that year the Easy Chair made money, gaining 5 per cent. In 2001, following the World Trade Center and Pentagon attacks, there was more devastation. People were desperate. Many of the portfolios that crossed my desk had lost half their value. But that year, the Easy Chair held steady. It didn't make any money, but it didn't lose any either. Its average annual return since 1997 dropped to 5.3 per cent.

Over the next decade, the Easy Chair rode out currency, accounting, real estate, and sovereign debt crises. In 2008, during the worst stock market crash since 1929, the Easy Chair suffered its first annual decline, losing 7 per cent for the year. In comparison, Canadian large company stocks as a group dropped 33 per cent, world stocks fell by 30.2 per cent, and US large company stocks lost 22.6 per cent of their value.

As I write this, halfway into 2011, with markets still off their early 2008 peak and interest rates still near historic lows, the Easy Chair sits there with an average annual compounded return of more than 7 per cent. The original $50,000 has grown over fifteen years to more than $140,000, with a minimum of oversight, cost, and anxiety.

Pretty close to what Eric Kirzner predicted.

From the beginning, the Easy Chair intrigued readers, even when the other portfolios were trouncing it. And as time went by, the questions and queries increased, and a number of my readers converted to the Easy Chair method. When David and I did a series of investment seminars between 2003 and 2005, most of the questions afterwards were about the Easy Chair. One lady took me aside and confided that she had put over $1 million into this simple little portfolio and "couldn't be happier." Even today, fifteen years after the first Easy Chair column was written, we still get questions about the little portfolio that could.

Of course, a lot has changed since 1997, when Kirzner designed the Easy Chair. On the plus side, RRSP accounts are less restrictive. In 1997, you could invest only 15 per cent of your RRSP money outside Canada. On the negative, the prime rate is half what it was then—3 per cent in 2011 compared to 6 per cent back then. Nonetheless, Kirzner still likes the way the portfolio is laid out. It's easy to understand, easy to manage and monitor, inexpensive to invest, and very doable for anyone.

"The average person has no chance of becoming educated enough to avoid all the pitfalls in the market," Kirzner states emphatically (and research bears him out). "And let's face it, most people really don't want to spend the kind of time required to build a truly diversified portfolio. We are entering a time when many people who were once willing to hand over their money to an adviser and trust them to build a sound portfolio aren't so sure that approach works. We've already seen how easy it is to gamble on a handful of stocks or funds and lose."

The beauty of the Easy Chair is how adjustable it is—just like a recliner that offers multiple positions for maximum comfort. You can build your own portfolio with a larger US percentage, a smaller cash portion, or a larger bond investment. That part doesn't matter. What has proven to be critical is that you pick an asset allocation and stick with it until there is a good reason to change. Most people won't need to change their asset allocation until they start getting within sight of retirement.

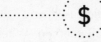

Case Study: Brady Wilson, 61

Brady Wilson switched to the Easy Chair in late 2000, following the tech meltdown. He'd read about it in one of our columns and came to a seminar where David and I talked about passive investing. "I had my doubts because there was so much in cash and bonds," he wrote in 2002, "but my friends have all seen their portfolios smashed and mine is still holding up well." Brady admits that he didn't experience the huge gains in 2006 and 2007 enjoyed by many mutual funds and stock portfolios because he had only 50 per cent of his money in the stock market. But when the financial crisis hit, his retirement savings were still afloat.

Brady partially retired in 2010. Financially, it made more sense for him to draw on his $182,000 RRSP at age sixty than to take his company pension early. Still, the only change he made to the original Easy Chair was to decrease his equity portion to 40 per cent (30 per cent Canada, 10 per cent United States) and increase the bonds to 40 per cent from 30 per cent. "My cash and bonds aren't earning much right now, but I have just enough interest income generated in my RRSP to top up my CPP and the money I get from working two days a week."

Brady's cash and bond portions (which amount to $109,200) are together returning 3.75 per cent, or about $4,100 a year. With the $11,500 he gets from the Canada Pension Plan and the $15,360 he earns working two days a week, his $31,000 income is sufficient to meet his needs. At sixty-five, he will stop drawing on his RRSP, stop working, and start collecting his company pension of $18,000 annually.

The Easy Chair will then be left to grow until he converts it to a RRIF at age seventy-one.

A decade and a half after the Easy Chair made its debut, the only thing that has changed in the portfolio are the products available. Wait a minute—there's actually one change I hate! The once simply and, to my mind, perfectly named index products are now confusingly called exchange-traded funds (ETFs), making them seem like mutual funds. Don't be fooled. Exchange-traded funds are not mutual funds, and despite their new name, most of them are still passive products that mirror a given index. (There

are, however, a host of new actively managed ETFs, but I'm betting they won't have any more luck beating the stock market over
time than their mutual fund cousins.)

If you are investing in the Easy Chair today there is only one
ETF cash option, which I will describe in chapter 14. Otherwise,
GICs make a better choice than money market funds. Because
interest rates are so low, the fees on money market funds eat up
much of the return. There are some good money market funds
available, but the best of them require large initial investments,
often $100,000 or more. With GICs there are no fees, and it is so
easy to have one in your portfolio and simply roll it over when it
comes due.

Back when the Easy Chair began, there were only two options
for bonds—buying them directly or buying a bond mutual fund.
Now you can buy bonds much more easily with exchange-traded
bond funds; there are a number of these available. These bond
ETFs hold baskets of bonds—just like bond mutual funds—but
because the management is passive (simply following a bond index)
rather than active (buying and selling), the fees are extremely low.
You can also buy bonds via index mutual funds at a slightly higher
fee than ETFs, and I'll detail the best ones available chapter 15.

The old TIPS 35 has been replaced by a number of very similar and equally low-fee ETFs. Again, because there is no manager
trying to beat the index or come out on top of a peer group, the
management fees on these funds are extremely low (between 0.17
and 0.35 per cent, compared to 2.5 per cent on average for actively
managed mutual funds). One of the best changes is that it is possible now to buy Canadian listed ETFs that mimic the major
US indices, such as the S&P 500 and the Dow Jones Industrial
Average. Most of them are hedged and expressed in Canadian
dollars—thus eliminating currency fluctuations.

In the next chapters, I will show you why passive investing
beats the active approach and how you can construct your own
Easy Chair portfolio.

CHAPTER 13

Going Passively

There are thousands of investment products, but there are only two basic ways to invest. Active investing involves buying and selling your holdings in an attempt to improve returns and to protect capital. Passive investing—the approach I recommend—is all about choosing an asset allocation, purchasing products that track an index, and then ensuring that the original allocation remains more or less the same over time. Let's look at each of these approaches in a bit more detail.

Active Investing

The aim of the game with active investing is to constantly tinker with your investments in order to produce the greatest return, find a sleeper of a stock, or jump to the sidelines before a market decline. Even if you own nothing but mutual funds in your RRSP and the closest you get to the stock market is to open your statement and look at the bottom line, you are almost certainly an active investor. That's because by far the majority of equity mutual funds are actively managed. That means trading, and sometimes a lot of it—buying shares of this company and selling shares of that one; watching market signals; taking profits; and moving in and out of sectors and asset classes as economic conditions, company fundamentals, and interest rates change or threaten to change.

Mutual fund managers want to beat the market and everyone else playing in the same arena. If you boast stellar returns, or lose less than everyone else during catastrophes, the bonuses will be large, advisers will recommend your fund to their clients, and investors will be attracted by ads proclaiming your fund's great performance. In a given year, even a conservatively managed fund could have a 30 per cent turnover of holdings. That means that if the fund holds one hundred stocks, thirty of them will change over the course of a year. Other funds might experience a 100 per cent turnover or more. The average turnover ranges from 70 to 85 per cent. One professional adherent of passive investing says bluntly, "Turnover kills." It costs a lot, not only in trading fees (which are far lower for fund managers than for regular folk) but also in time, staff, and research.

The basic idea behind active trading is that mutual fund managers want to get rid of yesterday's news and buy into tomorrow's big idea before anyone else does. And of course, absolutely everyone—from Joe Blow to Warren Buffett—wants to buy low and sell high. The problem is that very, very few can do it on any given day. And even fewer can do it on a sustained basis. We have known this since 1602, when the Dutch East India Company issued the first share offering on the Amsterdam Stock Exchange. Even so, half a millennium later an entire industry is built on the hope of achieving that rare feat—beating the market over time. This was what Bernie Madoff was supposedly doing before his calamitous fall. The wondrous returns he promised his clients—a 12 per cent annual gain on low-risk, supposedly cash-like investments when interest rates were almost zero—were ridiculous, and of course, it all proved to be a con. Still, the pursuit continues, generating trillions in fees and employing millions worldwide. But the focus on beating the market doesn't accomplish the most important financial management jobs very well—to enhance the investor's bottom line, minimize losses, maximize gains, and preserve capital.

It used to be that mutual funds were simple creatures to understand. Back in the 1970s, when they really started becoming popular, they were touted as the great investor leveller, a way of allowing ordinary people to invest in the stock and bond markets without needing scads of money. It made perfect sense to purchase a basket of stocks and bonds managed by a professional instead of trying to put together such a portfolio yourself. Mutual funds gave us access to the same wealth-building tools and expertise previously enjoyed only by the rich.

In 1978, the *Financial Times of Canada* conducted its first survey of mutual funds and found 144 to choose from. Most fell into one of four categories: equity (or large cap) funds, which were investing in Canada's largest companies; fixed income funds, which were investing in a mix of bonds; guaranteed income funds, which were primarily holding GICs, treasury bills, and other low- or zero-risk investments; and a handful of balanced funds, which held a mix of cash, bonds, and stocks.

The industry made investing in mutual funds easy. Purchasing units of a fund through an investment adviser appeared to be "free." (In reality, there were—and are—fees to pay, but it wasn't obvious to average folks saving for their retirement.) Later, when the big banks bought or created their own investment firms and discount brokerages, it became possible to purchase virtually any mutual fund available, so investors were no longer limited to the specific families of funds offered by whatever brokerage firm or mutual fund company they were working with.

Mutual funds became such a foundation of retirement savings plans that many consumers failed to realize these funds were only vehicles to invest in other products. I wish I had a buck for every time someone said to me, "I don't invest in the stock market. I buy mutual funds."

Over the last twenty-five years, mutual funds have multiplied

like weeds in an untended garden. As the second decade of the
twenty-first century saw first light, the number of funds available
in Canada ballooned to more than fifteen thousand (this includes
the segregated funds sold by insurance companies). There are
now funds in a myriad of categories and styles: segregated, tax-
efficient, growth, tactical, labour-sponsored, index, target date,
hedge, pure, sector, corporate class, and on and on. There are
funds so risky I break into a sweat just reading their holdings.
There are funds so conservative they resemble the large pension
plans of yore, when the primary investments were bonds and
GICs—nary a hockey team, shopping mall, or toll road in sight.
There are even funds of funds, in which one mutual fund holds a
bunch of other mutual funds.

The bottom line is that today, it is as difficult to select a portfolio of top-performing mutual funds as it is to pick a good-quality
stock portfolio. I don't have an issue with there being lots of choice
in the mutual fund marketplace. After all, there are thousands of
car and truck models to choose from. The problem is that most
investors lack the tools to evaluate the quality of the funds they
buy. With a car, you can at least test drive it to make sure it runs,
is comfortable, and suits your needs before you buy it. Of course
there are lemons, but most people have the basic tools necessary
to select a car that works for them. It's a very different story with
mutual funds. By the time you figure out a fund is a pooch, it's too
late, and deferred sales charges may keep you from getting out.

Unfortunately, there are far more bad funds than good ones.
Studies by the research firm DALBAR find that as many as 75
per cent of all equity and bond mutual funds do not beat or match
the performance of their benchmark indices over time. If you are
paying money (a fee) to someone to manage your fund, you should
at least expect that fund to beat its benchmark index. Otherwise,
why not just buy the index itself and avoid the fee?

My own observations, after fifteen years of writing about
investing, back up those studies. I've rarely seen a portfolio where

the mutual funds did any better than the simple mix of investments in the Easy Chair. Usually it isn't even close. Furthermore, those portfolios tend to drop faster and farther than the broader market during downturns, and recover more slowly during good times. The drag is caused by fees, as well as by the inability of money managers to guess (of course, fund managers will never say they "guess") correctly over time.

This is the crux of the matter. If the smart, highly paid fund managers, with their crack statisticians, fancy computer programs, and dedicated research teams, are unable to beat the market 75 per cent of the time, how is the average investor going to do it?

To be fair, there are some excellent mutual funds out there with top performance and easily justified fees. The first problem is finding them. Unless you have the skills to evaluate these funds, you are reliant on an adviser telling you what to buy. The best-quality funds may not even be offered to you because the commissions are not as high as those paid by lower-quality funds. The second problem is that good funds can change, sometimes dramatically. Managers come and go, firms merge, and funds are consolidated. One of the very first mutual funds I purchased changed names seven times in fifteen years before I got rid of it. Most of the savviest analysts follow specific fund managers. But how is the average person going to do that? Many funds list a team of fund managers, rather than one individual.

Finally, equity mutual funds tend to perform best against their benchmarks during hot stock markets. When markets are rising, people pile in, only to discover that their funds don't hold up nearly as well during flat, declining, or crashing markets.

Passive Investing

Let's say you don't like the 1 in 4 odds of landing a winning mutual fund. And let's assume you don't have the time, tools, or knowledge to assemble a well-diversified stock portfolio. If that's your situation, your very best and cheapest option is to become a passive investor. You will closely match the performance of the market using exchange-traded funds. And while you do it, you'll be paying the minimum fees possible.

At its essence, passive investing is a very, very simple process of picking an asset allocation, such as the Easy Chair or some variation of it, then investing your money in a small number of passive products (those exchange-traded funds). After that there is little to do except contribute new money, reinvest dividend or interest income, and make sure the original percentages remain more or less the same.

Doing little or nothing is a foreign concept to most investors. The financial services industry has done a brilliant job of convincing us that active management is the only way to go.

William F. Sharpe is a Nobel Prize–winning economist whose work on evaluating investment risk is the foundation of risk management today. After a lifetime of research, he concluded that "after costs, the return on the average actively managed dollar will be less than the return on the average passively managed dollar for any time period. The proof is embarrassingly simple and uses only the most rudimentary notions of simple arithmetic." When a man of Sharpe's credentials states unequivocally that passive beats active, and repeats it frequently, it is time to sit up and pay attention.

But if passive investing is so easy, cheap, and clearly superior, why doesn't everyone follow that path? Partly it's because of who we are as people. We tend to undervalue simplicity and overvalue complexity. We look at the trappings rather than the essence. We adore flash and glitz and hopeful projections. And we think that if something is easy to do, it must be worth less than something that is difficult and demands large amounts of expertise and training.

Passive investing is simple and easy to accomplish. And more than that, passive investing is boring. It is the Practical Pig style of growing your money—patiently putting one brick upon another, building an investment house that won't get blown down by the big bad wolf. There's no sex appeal in passive investing; you don't "play" the market or "take a flyer" on a stock.

Still, passive investing through a mix of ETFs won't totally shield you from the ups and downs of the market. When stocks like Nortel Networks plummet from $124 a share in 2000 to 43 cents in 2002, they drag the entire market down with them, and your index investment will also take a hit. When financials crash in the wake of an event like the subprime mortgage fiasco, your index investment will take a hit. But during those times, you have ballast in your portfolio to keep things on an even keel. That ballast is not only cash and bonds but also the discipline of rebalancing, which tells you to prune at peaks and buy at dips.

Cash and bonds, of course, are vulnerable to interest rate swings. When bond yields dropped to historic lows in 2008 and 2009, the yield on the bond portion of your portfolio would have declined also. And when interest rates scraped the bottom of the barrel during the same period, your cash investments wouldn't have produced much of a gain.

But historically during such times, the equity portion of your portfolio is strong. When equities droop, cash and bonds take up the slack. And when cash and bonds droop, equities generally take up the slack. It doesn't always work that way, but over time it usually does. That's why an investor who invests passively with a handful of ETFs, rebalances his or her portfolio from time to time, and reinvests dividend and interest income will ride out most of the market turbulence.

Passive investing has four components:

1. Decision: Select an asset allocation (or decide how
                    many eggs you'll put in each of your baskets).
2. Action: Purchase ETFs for equities and bonds, and
                    GICs for cash.
3. Discipline: Ignore the stock market noise.
4. Housekeeping: Reinvest dividend and interest income and
                    rebalance occasionally.

The next step in the Count On Yourself process is to take a closer look at some products that will suit most investors, and to see how to fit them into your own passive portfolio.

CHAPTER 14

Your Portfolio Building Blocks, Part 1— Exchange-Traded Funds

Years ago, the late Paul Newman, he of the stunning blue eyes and insouciant stare, was asked by a gossip columnist if he'd ever been tempted to stray from his wife, actress Joanne Woodward. The handsomest man of his generation could have had his pick of the female world. But Newman simply smiled and said, "Why would I go out for hamburger when I have steak at home?"

With apologies to Newman, I'm going to steal his comment and apply it to the investment universe. If you can have invest-ment steak at home, why would you bother going out for ground beef? Exchange-traded funds (ETFs) are steak for your portfo-lio, while actively managed mutual funds are, for the most part, ground beef. ETFs give you a lot less fat for your money. Not only are they cheaper—the management fees (MERs) of the ones I am recommending start as low as 0.07 per cent, most are well under 0.5 per cent (compared to the MERs for mutual funds, which average 2.5 per cent) and they produce a better result. As we saw in the previous chapter, roughly 75 per cent of mutual funds fail to outperform their comparable benchmark index over time. That's a staggering figure. The ETFs I'm recommending match their benchmark index almost 100 per cent of the time.

If you have only a 25 per cent chance of doing better than a given index—and you are going to pay through the nose for that underperformance—why wouldn't you just buy a piece of the index itself with an exchange-traded fund? The answer is simply that most people still don't know it's possible to invest by purchasing units of an index. Although ETFs have become much more popular, many people still don't know about them because, until recently, these funds paid no sales fees to financial advisers or their firms.

The majority of financial advisers, whether they work for mutual fund companies or investment firms, earn commissions, or fees, on the products they sell. Even salaried advisers employed by banks are still indirectly tied to the fees generated by what they recommend. You can bet that if a bank investment adviser spent all of his or her time funnelling clients into exchange-traded funds—which generate no sales fees—there would be some sharp words from on high. Over the years, I've known many advisers who left banks and investment firms because of the pressure to sell more expensive products to their clients rather than cheaper, but equally appropriate, investments. (Note that some ETFs are now offering fees to advisers, and of course that pushes up the cost for the investor.)

Although there are many excellent individuals in the investment business, the structure of compensation in most firms does not encourage them to push low-fee investment products. If they want to do that, they will have to strike out on their own and charge clients on a fee-for-service or fee-only basis. I do recommend that you try to find such professionals, but the difficulty is that fewer than 2 per cent of all advisers operate on this basis. Another roadblock is that advisers or financial planners licensed to sell mutual funds may not be licensed to sell stocks. Since ETFs are listed on exchanges like stocks, advisers need a broker's licence to sell them to clients.

> After years of buying supposedly "free" mutual funds,
> investors are highly resistant to paying out of pocket for
> investment advice.

There's a category of advisers called wealth managers, but most require you to have investable assets of $500,000 or more, and the price of entry for the top managers is $1 million or more. Even if you have this kind of money, most high-net-worth money advisers don't recommend ETFs. A passive approach hardly justifies the fees these managers charge (usually between 1 and 1.5 per cent of the assets under management) for research, analysis, and the other trappings of active management.

Fortunately, you can buy ETFs yourself through any discount brokerage without using middlemen. And if you don't feel confident doing this on your own, then search for an adviser who will do it for you on a fee-only basis. Or once you've settled on your asset allocation and your basket of ETFs, go to the bank where you have your brokerage account and get some assistance. If you already know what you want to buy and make that clear to whoever's helping you, the bank will still make money because you'll pay a trading fee to make your purchases.

Exchange-Traded Funds

Exchange-traded funds (ETFs) are the basis of the Count On Yourself low-fee, low-stress, comprehensible investing strategy. ETFs are suitable for investors of any age or at any stage. They work for beginners as well as those with larger investment accounts. They are great products for RRSPs, RESPs, RRIFs, RDSPs, and non-registered investment accounts. There are now thousands of ETFs available around the world. But remember to keep it simple, smarty. KISS! You don't need to invest in exotic, far-flung countries or load up on niche sectors like precious metals. All you require are two to four broad-based ETFs, a regular investment plan over time, and a bit of discipline for occasional portfolio housekeeping.

Pros:
- Very low management fees (MERs) because there is no stock picking or market analysis.
- Returns closely mirror a given index itself.
- No sales commissions (front-end loads or deferred sales charges).
- Transparent returns, which make ETFs far easier to understand than mutual funds.
- Easy to purchase (bought and sold like stocks through any discount brokerage).
- Two to four broad-based ETFs give you good diversification for a very low price.

Cons:
- Each purchase must be made through a discount brokerage unless you are paying an adviser/broker to do this part for you (in which case, expect to pay a fee in the range of 1 to 1.5 per cent of your portfolio's value, or an hourly rate based on the work involved).
- In most cases trading fees will apply for every transaction— a disadvantage if you have only a small amount of money to invest each month and don't qualify for the lowest trading fees (but there are ways around this, which I'll explain later).
- Interest or dividend income is not automatically reinvested, except for one family of ETFs.
- There is only one cash-like ETF, so if you want a cash investment the best option is to purchase GICs.
- When the stock market is hopping and everyone is into gold, real estate, or high-tech, you may be tempted to

stray from your broad-based ETFs into stocks or mutual funds to grab those short-term winners.

It's worth reviewing here that ETFs are "copies" of a given index. In some cases, they actually hold/own all the stocks or bonds in that index. In other cases, especially with ETFs that mimic larger or international indices, they use products called derivatives instead of the stocks themselves to copy the components of the index. Think of this as the difference between talking to someone in person and talking on the phone while holding a picture of that person. A slightly different path but a similar result.

An index is simply a basket of stocks or bonds that serves as a barometer for all or part of a stock market in a specific country or an entire region. Here is a selection of the main stock, or equity, indices:

INDEX	COUNTRY	WHAT'S IN IT
S&P/TSX 60	Canada	60 of Canada's largest companies
S&P/TSX Composite	Canada	Roughly 220 of Canada's largest companies
Dow Jones Industrial Average	United States	30 of America's largest "blue chip" companies, excluding utilities and transportation stocks
S&P 500	United States	500 of America's largest companies
Russell 2000	United States	2,000 small- and mid-sized companies
NASDAQ 100	United States	100 of America's largest technology companies
MSCI Europe	Europe	The major stock indices of 17 European countries
MSCI EAFE	Europe, Australia and the Far East	The major indices of the countries in those regions
MSCI Emerging Markets	Developing world	The major indices of 25 countries, including China, India, South Korea, Russia, Brazil, Mexico, etc.

Each index has criteria to determine which stocks qualify for inclusion. Because the *rules* dictate if a stock belongs in the index, the whole process is passive. In other words, there is no investment manager saying, "I like this gold company better than that one." Or, "It's time to move out of financials." Indices can be constructed in different ways. Some are based on the value of outstanding shares in the marketplace (called a capitalization-weighted index), while others are based on share price (called a price-weighted index). Still others, such as the RAFI indices, take a number of factors into account, including a company's size, sales, and dividends. You don't need to worry about any of this, though, because for the Count On Yourself plan, I am focusing only on the broadest indices. What's more, while there is a lively debate about which selection criteria produce the best barometer for a given market, the variations in how the indices are constructed won't affect you nearly as much as fees will in terms of your portfolio's performance.

There are over two hundred ETFs listed on the Toronto Stock Exchange, and more than sixteen hundred listed in the United States. You can pick up most major newspapers and find the ETFs I am recommending below in the same place you find stocks. Each ETF has a ticker symbol, and you can use that to look it up online or in print. In Canada, the three main providers of passive ETFs have been the following:

- iShares—managed by BlackRock Asset Management Canada
- BMO—managed by the Bank of Montreal
- Claymore—managed by Claymore Investments

But recently some new entrants have appeared, including PowerShares and Horizons, and by the time you read this, the US giant Vanguard and possibly RBC will be in the game, with others sure to follow.

These next tables are my top picks for creating your own passive (or index) portfolio. These ETFs all have tiny fees, closely follow or track their respective indices, and offer broad diversification. All are listed on the Toronto Stock Exchange (TSX). I am including a number of ETF options in the two major categories—Canadian large cap and US large cap—but you only need to pick one for Canada and one for the United States. They will give you excellent diversification at a low price.

Canadian Large Cap (Large Company) ETFs

This group of ETFs is focused on larger companies like the banks, big utilities, telecoms such as Bell and Rogers, and larger retailers like Shoppers Drug Mart, as well as major companies in the real estate, energy, and mining sectors. In the good old dot-com days, it was said that big companies grow slowly, so if you want to turbo-charge your portfolio you should go with smaller ones. While that is true during certain (but not all) time periods, big companies pay dividends. And they tend to increase those dividends over time. I love dividends as a relatively low-risk way to boost your investment return.

FUND	SYMBOL	INDEX	PROVIDER	MER (PER CENT)
Horizons S&P/TSX 60 Index ETF	HXT	S&P/TSX 60 Total Return Index	Horizons	0.07
BMO Dow Jones Canada Titans 60 Index ETF	ZCN	Dow Jones Canada Titans 60 Index	BMO	0.15
iShares S&P/TSX 60 Index Fund	XIU	S&P/TSX 60 Index	iShares	0.17
iShares S&P/TSX Capped Composite Index Fund	XIC	S&P/TSX Capped Composite Index	iShares	0.26
PowerShares Canadian Dividend Index ETF	PDC	Indxis Select Canadian Dividend Index	Invesco Trimark	0.50

FUND	SYMBOL	INDEX	PROVIDER	MER (PER CENT)
iShares S&P/TSX Equity Income Index Fund	XEI	S&P/TSX Equity Income Index	iShares	0.55
Claymore Canadian Fundamental Index ETF	CRQ	FTSE RAFI Canada Index	Claymore	0.72

*MERs do change, so check before you invest.

I must apologize for the number of ETFs in the table. Although I believe in competition and choice for the consumer, the ETF world is getting crowded. By the time this book is published, there will almost certainly be more. I haven't included every Canadian ETF available, in the interests of keeping things simple, but this list does cover my picks for a broad-based and inexpensive Canadian investment. You only need to choose one of the above funds.

You'll note that there are more indices listed above than the basic group I described earlier. With the proliferation of ETFs, we've also seen an explosion in the number of indices. Each ETF provider will argue the merits of their particular index. Yes, there will be variation in return. Don't worry about it. You only need one ETF for your Canadian investment. Regular investing and portfolio housekeeping are more important than small return differences.

The first three funds (and the index they track) are similar to one another and include Canada's largest companies. The first, the Horizons ETF (launched in late 2010), is somewhat different, however, because it tracks the S&P/TSX 60 Total Return Index, which includes dividends. Don't try to compare the regular TSX 60 Index with the Total Return Index. The latter will always be higher because dividends are factored in. Why have they done this? Well, the main reason is that the Horizons folk are carving their own niche with tax-efficient ETFs, which no one else is currently offering. By incorporating the dividends and using a bit of money-management sleight of hand (called a total return swap, if you want to know), this fund protects you from getting taxed on the annual dividend payments. It's like a dividend reinvestment plan with a twist.

The companies in the S&P/TSX 60 Index pay dividends, of course, and the other ETFs that track this index pay them accordingly. But the HXT folds the dividends into the unit price, making the fund more tax efficient. The unit price of HXT will appear to increase more rapidly than that of other S&P/TSX 60 Index ETFs because it tracks the S&P/TSX 60 Total Return Index. Essentially, the dividends become part of the price growth of your investment. This is handy if you're concerned about tax and are investing outside RRSPs or other registered accounts. It's also handy if you are a lazy investor and don't want to worry about physically reinvesting your dividends. But if your investment is inside a tax-sheltered account such as an RRSP, a TFSA, an RDSP, or even an RESP (where the student is taxed on the income), you don't really care about the tax efficiency.

You might still care about HXT's very skinny MER of 0.07 per cent, however, which means more of your money is working for you from the get-go because less of it is going to fees. On the downside, Horizons' passive ETFs are new and the tax-efficiency sleight of hand is also new to the Canadian ETF game. Generally, I prefer products that have a proven track record or adhere to a well-tested strategy. However, Horizons does have a longer track record with other kinds of ETFs.

The fourth fund, XIC, tracks the S&P/TSX Capped Composite Index, which follows the broader Canadian market. Funds five and six, PDC and XEI, track indices that focus on companies paying the highest dividends.

The last one, CRQ, is the odd man out, since the index it tracks is quite different. As I explained earlier, the RAFI indices take more factors into account, and many feel that is a superior method for creating an index. Normally, I wouldn't have included an ETF with an MER of 0.72 per cent, but so far, this particular ETF has outperformed the others in some time frames.

> Dividend reinvestment plans (DRIPs) automatically rein-
> vest dividends back into the stock, mutual fund, or ETF.
> DRIPs allow you to acquire more shares or units without
> any effort or trading fees. Most mutual funds and many of
> the larger listed companies offer this feature, but DRIPs
> are relatively new to the ETF business.

You will also note the word *capped* in the S&P/TSX Composite Index above. This indicates that no one company can account
for more than a certain portion of the index. The rise and fall of
Nortel Networks and other high-tech high flyers is the reason.
At its peak, Nortel, a higher-risk technology company, accounted
for a ridiculous 35 per cent of the value of Canada's major stock
market index. Its share price was driven to unreasonable heights
by the mania for high-tech, and this inflated share price bloated
its value, and thus its impact, on the index. Capping an index is
a good idea in a country like Canada, where there isn't the same
broad choice of companies that exist on larger stock exchanges. It
eliminates the possibility of a single stock or sector rising up to
become a bubble in the index.

Don't worry about the intricacies of which index is better. Any
one of these ETFs listed will serve you well as your Canadian
investment.

US Large Cap (Large Company) Equity ETFs

All the US ETFs listed below are hedged to the Canadian dollar.
This means the currency factor is neutralized. Some people want
to invest in currency *and* stocks when they invest internationally.
Those who do profit when the Canadian dollar sinks because
their international investments are worth more once translated
back into loonies. But when the dollar rises, as we've seen over the
past two years, the reverse is true.

There's nothing wrong with including currency as part of your investment strategy, if you are prepared for the ups and downs. Sophisticated investors and mutual fund managers try to use currency fluctuations to increase their profits. But currencies are as unpredictable as interest rates and stock prices, and no one can accurately predict where a given currency is headed. For example, at the beginning of 2011, I interviewed a number of experts who expected the loonie to be worth $1.15 against the US dollar by the summer of 2011. I am writing this as the leaves are turning and the loonie sits at $0.96.

Currency fluctuations can also introduce considerable risk and volatility into a portfolio. For most investors, keeping US investments in Canadian dollars reduces the unknown and keeps things simple. KISS!

ETF	SYMBOL	INDEX	PROVIDER	MER (PER CENT)
Horizons S&P 500 Index	HXS	S&P 500 (Total Return) Index	Horizons	0.15
BMO US Equity	ZUE	Dow Jones US Large Cap Index	BMO	0.22
BMO Dow Jones Industrial Average Index	ZDJ	Dow Jones Industrial Average Index	BMO	0.23
iShares S&P 500 Index Fund	XSP	S&P 500 Index	iShares	0.25
Claymore US Fundamental Index	CLU	FTSE RAFI US 1000 Index	Claymore	0.72

There are many more ETFs now that track US indices. I've picked this group because they are simple and broad. They are all slightly different and will perform somewhat differently over time. You only need one of the above to get good exposure to the broad US stock market.

There are a couple of new indices here in addition to the "classics," the S&P 500 and the Dow Jones. The RAFI 1000 is a broader index than the S&P 500 because it contains one thousand companies. The Dow Jones US Large Cap (or large company) is similar to the Dow Jones except there are more companies— ninety-plus instead of thirty—and companies are selected for the index based on the value of outstanding shares instead of the price of the shares.

The case for buying an ETF that tracks an index of more and smaller companies is that the share prices of small- and medium-sized companies often grow more quickly than that of the behemoths. This can be true, but it isn't always. The thirty-company Dow, with no transportation or utility companies, is often criticized as a dinosaur, but it has outperformed the S&P 500 in recent years quite handily, in part because the dividend payments are higher.

Understanding Dividends

Many companies pay dividends. Let's say you buy a stock for $50 a share and it pays an annual dividend of $2.50, or roughly 62 cents every three months. That's 5 per cent of the share price ($2.50 ÷ $50 × 100 = 5 per cent). So we would say that the stock has a 5 per cent dividend yield. Most companies in the indices I'm mentioning pay dividends. When you buy an index with an ETF, you will get a dividend payment based on how the companies are weighted in the index. The largest companies usually pay larger dividends, so the dividend yield will be higher if you pick one of the Dow Jones ETFs than if you choose XSP or CLU (which hold five hundred and one thousand companies, respectively).

Here's how the some of the US indices compare in terms of dividend yield as of June 2011:

INDEX	NUMBER OF COMPANIES	DIVIDEND YIELD (PER CENT)
Dow Jones Industrial Average	30	2.56
Dow Jones US Large Cap	Around 90	2.05
S&P 500	500	1.79
RAFI 1000	Around 1000	1.50

As you can see, indices with larger (and fewer) companies pay higher dividends. The beauty of dividend-paying companies is that they usually increase their dividends over time. Of course, stuff happens in the stock market, and sometimes companies cut or even eliminate dividends. In 2009, when all hell was breaking loose over the subprime mortgage mess, GE—a dividend stalwart if ever there was one—cut its payment by 68 per cent. That was a shocker.

However, when you buy an index full of dividend-paying companies, you are also buying some protection from disaster when a single stock or even an entire sector falters. Some of the companies might do what GE and the US banks did during the financial crisis. But since you own the whole index when you buy an ETF, cuts won't affect you as much as they would if you owned just one or two individual stocks in the index.

Similarly, actively managed mutual funds will take a big hit if managers bet wrong on a handful of stocks in a given index. Just before the technology and financial crises, many mutual funds had loaded up on companies in those areas, betting the run would continue. They were trounced as a result.

Global Equity ETFs

Should you buy an international ETF as well as a US ETF? You really don't need to. You can get excellent diversification with Canadian and US broad-based ETFs because the big companies in the major indices do business all over the world. In fact, some of the bigger companies actually earn the majority of their revenue from outside the United States and Canada. McDonald's and Colgate-Palmolive (more than 50 per cent), Coke (70 per cent), and Research in Motion (60 per cent) are among many North American companies with a large part of their revenues in places such as Europe, Latin America, India, and the Far East.

However, if you feel you must, you can certainly add more exposure to Europe and the Far East with any of the three ETFs below:

ETF	SYMBOL	INDEX	PROVIDER	MER (PER CENT)
MSCI EAFE Index Fund (hedged)	XIN	MSCI EAFE Index	iShares	0.50
BMO International Equity Index Fund (hedged)	ZDM	Dow Jones Developed Markets Index (not including North America)	BMO	0.46
Claymore International Fundamental Index Fund (not hedged)	CIE	FTSE RAFI Developed 1000 Index (not including North America)	Claymore	0.66

You'll notice that the first two funds are hedged to the Canadian dollar, as are all the US ETFs. Many experts now feel this is unnecessary when international index baskets contain many different currencies. Additionally, these hedging strategies—when applied to multiple currencies, compared to a single currency like the US dollar—can actually act as a drag on return. You'll often find that international ETFs have difficulty matching, or tracking, the performance of their benchmark indices (which is the whole point of buying an ETF) if they are hedged to neutralize currency fluctuations.

The "to hedge or not to hedge" issue is another reason I believe most investors need to buy only one broad US ETF and one broad Canadian ETF. But if you do want extra international exposure, the research I have seen so far favours a non-hedged ETF. By the time you are reading this book, non-hedged versions of the iShares and BMO ETFs may be available.

Fixed Income

Happily, there are now many bond ETFs available. It used to be that the only alternative to bond mutual funds was buying the bonds directly. But in these days of low interest rates, the fee to buy bonds really cuts into your yield, just as the MER on bond mutual funds takes a chunk out of your return. For these reasons, bond ETFs are more attractive than ever.

Today, there are bond ETFs for everything from government and corporate bonds to bonds from many countries. I winnowed down the list, eliminating any ETFs that included the following:

1. High-yield bonds. The yield will definitely be higher but bonds have a specific job to do in a passive portfolio, and that is to provide income safely. High-yield bonds are far riskier.
2. Longer-term bonds. The yield will also be higher here, but as interest rates rise, longer-term bonds will be less valuable and the price of these ETFs may decline.
3. MERs over 0.5 per cent.

ETF	SYMBOL	INDEX	PROVIDER	MER (PER CENT)
Claymore 1–5 Year Laddered Government Bond ETF	CLF	DEX 1–5 Year Laddered Government Bond Index	Claymore	0.17
BMO Short Provincial Bond Index ETF	ZPS	DEX Short Term Provincial Bond Index	BMO	0.25

ETF	SYMBOL	INDEX	PROVIDER	MER (PER CENT)
iShares DEX All Corporate Bond Index Fund	XCB	DEX All Corporate Bond Index	iShares	0.25
PowerShares 1–5 Year Laddered Investment Grade Corporate Bond Index ETF	PSB	DEX Investment Grade 1–5 Year Laddered Corporate Bond Index	Invesco Power-Shares	0.25
iShares DEX Short-Term Bond Index Fund	XSB	DEX Short Term Bond Index	iShares	0.26
Claymore 1–5 Year Laddered Corporate Bond ETF	CBO	DEX 1–5 Year Corporate Bond Index	Claymore	0.27
BMO Aggregate Bond Index ETF	ZAG	DEX Universe XM Bond Index	BMO	0.28
Claymore Advantaged Canadian Bond ETF	CAB	DEX DLUX Capped Bond Index	Claymore	0.32

Again, I apologize for the long list of options. Actually this list could easily be doubled, as there are many more bond ETFs available. BMO, for example, offers a complete range of all-corporate bonds, from very short to long term.

The good news is that any of the bond ETFs above would be a good choice for your passive ETF portfolio. You only need one to get a piece of a broadly diversified group of bonds. The first two funds track a Canadian government bond index. The second two track a broad corporate bond index. And the final four are a mix of both. Government bonds are the safest but will give you a lower yield. Corporate bonds are somewhat riskier but have a higher yield. However, the ETFs I've listed hold only higher-grade corporate bonds and so the risk of loss is fairly low.

Any of this group would be a good choice for the fixed income part of your portfolio, but my recommendation right now, for most portfolios, would be either a corporate bond ETF or one that has both government and corporate bonds to get you a higher, but still safe, yield.

More Diversification?

The two areas investors accustomed to buying mutual funds may feel are lacking in my simple ETF portfolios are technology and small companies. But does more diversification really help? If you'd invested 10 per cent of your passive portfolio in US small company stocks, you would have actually reduced your average annual return over the last three and five years. Over ten years, your increase would have been 0.9 per cent, and it would have been only 0.1 per cent for twenty years. Those figures don't include trading fees, so once you add them it is probably a wash over time, and possibly a loss.

Of course, who knows about the next three, five, and ten years? But the figures go to show that you don't necessarily need many products to get a decent and relatively low-risk return.

As for improving diversification, more than 21 per cent of companies in the S&P 500 are in the information technology and telecommunications sectors, so once again you're getting a fair bit of diversification just by buying broad-based Canadian and US ETFs. Of course, the next ten years may not be the same as the last ten. And if you want to hedge your bets by adding one or more specialty ETFs, you certainly can. But if you do, each one represents one more item to monitor in your portfolio.

Here are a group of ETFs I like for technology and for smaller companies:

TECHNOLOGY ETF	SYMBOL	INDEX	PRO-VIDER	MER (PER CENT)
PowerShares QQQ Index ETF (hedged)	QQC	NASDAQ 100 Index	Invesco Power-Shares	0.32
iShares NASDAQ 100 Index Fund (hedged)	XQQ	NASDAQ 100 Index	iShares	0.35
BMO NASDAQ 100 Equity Index ETF (hedged)	ZQQ	NASDAQ 100 Index	BMO	0.35

SMALL- TO MID-COMPANY ETF	SYMBOL	INDEX	PROVIDER	MER (PER CENT)
iShares Russell 2000 Index Fund (US, hedged)	XSU	Russell 2000 Index	iShares	0.35
iShares S&P/TSX Small Cap Index Fund (Canada)	XCS	S&P/TSX Small Cap Index	iShares	0.55

There are many more ETFs that slice and dice the pie in all kinds of ways, but if you are looking for a solid, simple portfolio you don't need them.

And there you have it—a recommended group of ETFs to choose from to build a low-fee, passive portfolio that will likely last you for most of your investing life. You can treat my lists like the options on a prix fixe menu—select one from each group and you're done! That means one Canadian ETF, one US ETF, and one bond ETF. Yes, it is *that* simple. In chapters 16, 17, and 18, I'll show you some sample portfolios that you can follow exactly or adapt according to your situation.

The next chapter explains an alternative way of index investing, which is a great option if you are just starting out, have a small amount of money to invest monthly, or simply don't want to bother with even a teeny bit of work to set up and manage your portfolio.

CHAPTER 15

Your Portfolio Building Blocks, Part 2—Index Mutual Funds

Fifteen years ago, passive (or index) investing hadn't really caught on with mutual funds. But today, every bank and most mutual fund companies, eager to get a piece of the increasingly popular ETF action, have a number of funds that attempt to mimic ETFs by replicating the performance of a given index. Put another way, these investment products are similar to ETFs but are managed by mutual fund companies.

Index mutual funds, unlike other mutual funds, are passive; there is no active management, no buying and selling, no guessing which way the investment winds are going to blow next. Like ETFs, these funds simply mirror an index as closely as possible. And as with ETFs, there are two main categories: equity (or stock) index mutual funds and those that hold only bonds. Like ETFs, equity index mutual funds replicate a broad stock market index, such as the S&P/TSX Composite or the Dow Jones Industrial Average. Bond index mutual funds mimic a bond index.

There are also sector index mutual funds that focus on specific market sectors, such as technology, agriculture, or energy. These funds also track, or mimic, the indices of those sectors. However, just as I recommended with the ETF approach in the previous chapter, two or three broadly based index mutual funds will provide enough diversification for most investors.

You might wonder why on earth I am talking about mutual funds after spending many chapters trying to convince you that they are a bad deal. It's a fair question. I am including them because, though I believe passive investing with ETFs will produce better results for the majority of investors, many people will never break the mutual fund habit.

I also want to offer an index mutual fund option with the sample portfolios I'm going to outline because they are a better fit for people who are contributing only a small amount to their RRSPs or other investment accounts—especially those who don't have enough bank business ($50,000 to $100,000 in assets and loans)—to qualify for lower fees of $6.95 to $9.95 per trade. If you are paying nearly $30 every time you buy ETF units, the costs are prohibitive for those with only a couple of hundred a month to invest. An index mutual fund portfolio is also a good choice for young parents starting RESPs for their kids, as well as a single person of any age who has a small portfolio, is making smaller contributions regularly, and doesn't qualify for lower trading fees.

I am also taking into consideration human nature and different situations. Index mutual funds are a little more convenient than ETFs because interest income and dividends are automatically reinvested. You can set up an automatic investment program with small purchases monthly. I should also say here that Claymore, which offers an entire range of ETFs, does have an automatic investment and dividend reinvestment program, so you can get the convenience of mutual funds at a lower cost. In time, I'm betting most ETF providers will have this option. Additionally, the Scotia iTrade brokerage announced in the summer of 2011 that no trading fees will be levied for ETF trades. That's a game changer and may signal the end of index mutual funds.

Some of you may be convinced of the passive approach but still want some handholding. If so, index mutual funds do pay fees to advisers, and they don't need to be licensed to sell stocks in order to help you create an index portfolio. Remember, ETFs are listed like stocks.

Finally, the major banks have most of the best index mutual funds, so it is quite straightforward to open an RRSP or get a bank adviser who is licensed to sell mutual funds to help you set up the portfolio. You may not get much advice or service after that, but quite frankly, you probably won't need it.

And then there are those who just don't want to be bothered with the slightly more work involved in an ETF portfolio. That's okay. In the end, if you follow the passive approach you will be far better off even if you do it with index mutual funds rather than the ETFs themselves. As time goes on, you can always switch to an ETF portfolio and save even more money.

Index mutual funds (at least the ones I am recommending) are passive. They do almost exactly what ETFs do. The difference is cost. Index mutual funds have higher management fees than ETFs. Even though there is no stock picking, trading, and research, they are still run by mutual fund companies.

To recap:

Pros:
- In most cases, no fees to buy or sell units, which keeps trading costs down.
- MERs (management expense ratios) of between 0.32 and 1 per cent (at least for the ones I am recommending), versus the industry average of 2.5 per cent for actively managed mutual funds.
- Automatic purchase plans that allow monthly purchases with as little as $25 per fund.
- Dividends and/or interest income reinvested automatically.
- Excellent diversification for an RRSP or RESP.

Cons:
- Higher fees than with an exchange-traded fund (ETF).
- May have a lower return than the index itself—again, because of those fees.
- Confusion of choice because of the proliferation of funds calling themselves index mutual funds (some of which have fees as high as regular mutual funds).

WARNING! An increasing number of index mutual funds are not passive at all. Instead of buying and selling stocks, the managers buy and sell indices. Let me be clear: I do not think actively managed index mutual funds are a good choice for most investors. Fees are higher, returns are likely to be lower over time, and the funds are beset by the same problems that plague regular mutual funds. While some actively managed mutual funds will do very well in certain markets, over time their managers won't do any better in predicting the economic or social changes that affect stocks worldwide.

Index Mutual Funds: The List

The funds listed in the pages that follow are the best choices for most index investors. You can get fancy by choosing funds that invest in different sectors and countries, but there is no reason. Just pick one broadly based Canadian and one broadly based US index mutual fund and you will have excellent diversification. Add to that a single bond index mutual fund and there's your portfolio!

I used several specific criteria to select the best funds for each of those three categories. It would be a good idea to double-check this information before you buy, however, as more funds may have been added and fees may have changed by the time this book comes off the press. My criteria were as follows:

1. MER of less than 1 per cent.
2. Minimum investment of $100 or less needed after initial purchase.
3. Three-star rating or better from morningstar.ca or *The Globe and Mail*'s globefund.com, both of which rank mutual funds. This rating indicates that the fund tracks its index closely, which is the whole intent of passive investing.
4. No front-end load fee or deferred sales charge.

Canadian Large Cap (Large Company) Index Mutual Funds

These index mutual funds will track one of the broader Canadian indices mentioned in the previous chapter. You will get dividend payments just as you would with an ETF, but in this case, the dividends will be reinvested for you, which is convenient.

INDEX MUTUAL FUND	INDEX	MER (PER CENT)	INITIAL/SUBSEQUENT INVESTMENT
TD Canadian Index-e	S&P/TSX Composite Index	0.32	$100/$100
Altamira Canadian Index	S&P/TSX 60 Index	0.64	$500/$50/$25*
RBC Canadian Index	S&P/TSX Composite Index	0.70	$1000/$25
TD Canadian Index	S&P/TSX Composite Index	0.86	$100/$100
Scotia Canadian Index	S&P/TSX Composite Index	0.99	$1000/$50

*$25 is the minimum amount if you sign up for Altamira's systematic investment plan and make regular monthly purchases.

You only need one of the above index mutual funds, and any of these will do nicely (though the lower the fee, the closer you will follow the returns of the index). The e-versions of the TD funds are great choices, but only if you have a TD Waterhouse discount brokerage account. You can't buy them through other brokerages.

Also, the minimum initial investment may affect your choice. While the Altamira and RBC funds are a bit cheaper than the TD fund (the non-e version), if you are starting with only $100 and want to invest right away, you will have to choose the more expensive TD Canadian Index with its 0.86 per cent MER. Or better yet, open a discount brokerage account at TD and buy their e-version with its 0.32 MER.

US Large Cap (Large Company) Index Mutual Funds

All the funds listed below are hedged to the Canadian dollar to neutralize currency fluctuations (as I explained in the previous chapter). Non-hedged versions are available for some; the MERs for these are in brackets. The hedged version protects you if the loonie keeps getting stronger against the US greenback. Choose this version if you don't want to worry about that possibility or about future volatility. However, since the loonie has been flying pretty high, you might want to choose the non-hedged version to take advantage if there is a drop. But recognize that with the non-hedged version, there may be more volatility over time.

In the end, though, it all comes down to simplicity, which is what a passive portfolio is all about. Don't switch to the hedged version if the loonie drops to ninety cents and then back to the non-hedged if it climbs above par. If your time frame is reasonably long—ten years or more—pick one version and stick with it. You don't want to be jumping in and out of your investments because of changes in currency.

INDEX MUTUAL FUND	INDEX	MER (PER CENT)	INITIAL/ SUBSEQUENT INVESTMENT
TD Dow Jones Average Index-e	Dow Jones Industrial Average	0.32	$100/$100
TD US Index Currency Neutral-e	S&P 500 Index	0.50 (0.34)	$100/$100
Altamira US Index	Dow Jones Industrial Index	0.86 (0.53)	$100/$100
Altamira US Currency Neutral Index	S&P 500 Index	0.64 (0.63)	$500/$50/$25*
RBC US Index Currency Neutral	S&P 500 Index	0.70 (0.71)	$1000/$25
TD US Index Currency Neutral	S&P 500 Index	0.86 (0.53)	$100/$100
TD Dow Jones Average Index	Dow Jones Industrial Index	0.86	$100/$100

*$25 is the minimum amount if you sign up for Altamira's systematic investment plan and make regularly monthly purchases.

How do you choose? Look at your situation. If you are TD customer, go with those funds. If you have your investment account elsewhere and have small amounts to invest, Altamira is a good option. If you have over $1,000 right now but only small amounts to invest subsequently, then either the RBC or the Altamira funds will work.

Bond Index Mutual Funds

There aren't many low-fee, top-performing options out there. In fact, when I sifted through all the bond index mutual funds available, I found only a few that met my criteria. Here they are:

INDEX MUTUAL FUND	INDEX	MER (PER CENT)	INITIAL/ SUBSEQUENT INVESTMENT
TD Canadian Bond Index-e (for those with TD accounts)	DEX Universe Bond Index	0.49	$100/$100
RBC Canadian Bond Index	DEX Universe Federal Bond Index	0.65	$1000/$25
TD Canadian Bond Index	DEX Universe Bond Index	0.81	$100/$100
Scotia Canadian Bond Index	DEX Universe Bond Index	0.84	$1000/$50

The offerings are thin on the ground, and I could find no fund tracking the shorter-term bond indices that met my criteria. I prefer shorter-term bonds right now because interest rates are far more likely to rise than fall. The return will be lower, but as rates rise, the bonds in the fund will be rolled over into higher-yielding bonds.

Still, for those wanting to follow the passive approach with index mutual funds rather than ETFs, either the TD or Scotia fund will give you excellent exposure to a broad bond index. These are the best way to buy bonds if you have smaller amounts of money to invest and insufficient "bank business" to qualify for lower trading fees.

Selecting three index mutual funds—one Canadian, one US, and one bond—will give you a well-diversified portfolio at a reasonable cost. Your dividends and interest income will be reinvested automatically, and you can set up automatic regular deposits.

Easy to do. Easy to understand. Such an index mutual fund portfolio won't perform quite as well as one created with cheaper ETFs, but it will beat most mutual fund portfolios, hands down.

Beyond the Basics

As I discussed in the previous chapter, adding other products to your passive portfolio isn't really necessary. But if you want a bit more diversification you could consider adding a technology, international, or small cap index mutual fund. There is a technology component to a broad index such as the S&P 500, but it certainly won't contain all the stocks listed on the NASDAQ, the tech-focused index. Similarly, a broad US index will have a strong international component because of the worldwide nature of large companies. Still, if you want a bit more global focus, I've listed some options.

There aren't a lot of choices because I only included index mutual funds with MERs of less than 1 per cent, a three-star ranking or better, and a low initial and subsequent investment.

US Equity—Technology Index Mutual Funds

Like the US index mutual funds, these technology funds come in hedged and non-hedged versions. The MER for the non-hedged version is in brackets. If you do choose to add a higher concentration of technology to your portfolio, just be sure you don't make it too large a percentage—5 to 10 per cent will do. Technology companies generally pay small or no dividends, and the stock prices tend to be more volatile, which increases your risk.

INDEX MUTUAL FUND	INDEX	MER (PER CENT)	INITIAL/ SUBSEQUENT INVESTMENT
TD NASDAQ Index-e (for those with TD brokerage accounts)	NASDAQ 100 Index	0.50 (0.34)	$100/$100
TD NASDAQ Index	NASDAQ 100 Index	0.99 (0.91)	$100/$100

International Equity Indices

If you want to add an international index mutual fund, I'd suggest you stick to the non-hedged version for funds with multiple currencies and the hedged version for anything with a single currency, like Europe or the United States. The MERs for the non-hedged versions are in brackets. As I discussed in the previous chapter, there is some debate about whether it adds value to neutralize the currency effect when you are dealing with a basket of currencies.

As I've said before, you don't really need an international fund to get exposure to the rest of the world; large Canadian and US companies do business all over the world and receive a good percentage (in some cases a majority) of their revenues from global operations. But if you want extra international exposure, here are some options:

INDEX MUTUAL FUND	INDEX	MER (PER CENT)	INITIAL/ SUBSEQUENT INVESTMENT
TD European Index-e (for those with TD brokerage accounts)	MSCI Europe Index	0.49 (0.4)	$100/$100
TD International Index-e (as above)	MSCI EAFE Index (Europe, Australia, and the Far East)	0.52 (0.50)	$100/$100
Altamira International Index	MSCI EAFE Index	0.64 (0.63)	$500/$50/$25*
RBC International Index	MSCI EAFE Index	0.69	$1000/$25
TD International Index†	MSCI EAFE Index	0.98	$100/$100

*$25 is the minimum amount if you sign up for Altamira's systematic investment plan.

†TD International Index does exist in a non-hedged version, but because the MER is over 1%, it doesn't meet the criteria for inclusion.

Cash

Money market funds used to be a great index-like place to invest in the cash asset class or simply to store cash you intend to invest later. Today, I don't recommend them because, with interest rates so low, fees eat up a good portion of your return. The average money market fund in Canada was returning less than 0.30 per cent when this book went to press. And some funds had returned nothing at all to their investors.

For cash-type investments, you are better off purchasing GICs and rolling them over with interest as they come due. It is easy and straightforward. As interest rates rise, you will benefit as long as you keep your term short. If interest rates approach historic levels or even spike above them, you can certainly lock in for longer time periods.

However, for index mutual fund investors who have chosen this route because their portfolios or monthly contributions are small, GICs don't entirely do the job because brokerage firms often have minimum investment amounts of $5,000 or more. It can take a while for you to build up that much cash if you are starting from scratch. If you fit this profile, consider ignoring GICs in the short term and treating bonds as your sole fixed income investment. Cash does have a place in your portfolio, especially as rates rise, but for newbie investors with beginning portfolios, KISS rules.

Now you have a handle on creating a passive (or index) portfolio with index mutual funds, and you understand why you might choose this approach over ETFs themselves. Next, we move on to deciding how to pick an asset allocation. Finally, I'll show you a series of sample portfolios that will fit a variety of situations.

CHAPTER 16

Lights! Camera! Action! Pick Your Asset Allocation

Now you have a selection of ETFs and index mutual funds to choose from to create your own easy-to-manage passive portfolio. The next step is to divvy up your money among the three major asset classes—cash, fixed income, and equities. I talked about asset allocation (spreading your investment eggs) in chapters 9 and 10. This is where we'll put it to work. Remember, the best way to produce a solid, lower-risk gain in your portfolio over time is to:

1. Create an asset allocation.
2. Rebalance occasionally to maintain that asset allocation.
3. Reinvest dividends and interest income (index mutual funds and one ETF family, Claymore, will do this automatically).
4. Forget about your portfolio until it's necessary to rebalance again (usually once a year or so).

Caution! Micromanaging will likely produce a lower gain. Research indicates that constantly tinkering with a portfolio and rebalancing multiple times a year actually reduces return because of increased trading fees. Also, investors who try to time the market or ride investment bandwagons inevitably fail over time. A far better way to take advantage of market and interest rate ups and downs is to follow the housekeeping practice of rebalancing.

How Do You Choose an Asset Allocation?

The industry's standard rule for asset allocation is to invest your age. In other words, spread your equity and fixed income (in this case, fixed income includes cash and bonds) eggs according to your age, like so:

- 30 years old: 30 per cent fixed income, 70 per cent equities
- 50 years old: 50 per cent fixed income, 50 per cent equities
- 65 years old: 65 per cent fixed income, 35 per cent equities

As a rule of thumb, invest your age isn't a bad one. It doesn't take into account all the factors we discussed earlier—time frame, situation, and temperament—but if you are new to investing (regardless of age) or are just beginning to take control of your investing life, this is a good place to start. You can easily vary it. Many younger investors who don't like risk, for instance, will be happier with less than 70 per cent in equities. Except for periods when the stock market is on a screaming tear, I have yet to meet a conservative investor who regrets the choice. With three major stock market meltdowns since 2000, erring on the conservative side has paid big dividends. If you are over sixty-five and feel even 35 per cent in the stock market is too rich, just drop that percentage and up the fixed income. You can always increase the amount in equities at a later date.

We've been told for decades that investing in equities, through either equity mutual funds or individual stocks, is the only way to achieve growth. The market has proven otherwise. It may be that we are heading into a long period of stability in the stock market, but it's equally likely that more instability is coming our way. Who knows? No one predicted the global turmoil, mismanagement, and downright fraud that has afflicted the market over the past decade, let alone events such as 9/11. Frankly it's better to assume that anything can and will happen. A relatively conservative asset allocation that is maintained regularly is the best defence against the unknown.

Look over the following scenarios to determine which asset allocation is right for you. You will probably find elements of your situation in a number of categories. Keep in mind the "invest your age" guideline above, but don't forget that age is actually less important than situation and temperament. And if you are uncertain, choose the less aggressive route, at least initially. Here's a range of least to most conservative types.

1: Least conservative

- You or your spouse has a workplace defined benefit pension plan that will provide 50 per cent or more of your retirement income.
- You have a workplace group RRSP or a defined contribution pension plan that is conservatively managed, has held up well during the recent market crashes, and is likely to provide 50 per cent or more of your retirement income.
- You are young with a very long time frame and no children.
- You like taking a few financial chances.
- You have time to ride out the market ups and downs (at least ten years).
- You have oodles of dough.

Defined benefit plans are so-called gold-plated pensions typically associated with civil servants, teachers, university and hospital workers, and employees of certain large corporations. A DB plan pays a guaranteed income on retirement based upon years of service and salary (usually in the last years of employment). Outside of government, DB plans are increasingly rare, and some DB plans are underfunded (meaning retirees may face a cut in benefits).

2: Mildly conservative

- You are willing to work past your ideal retirement age if your RRSP doesn't turn out to be as large as you would like.
- You have a partner who is contributing to a workplace pension and expects to have twenty to twenty-five years of contributions by retirement.
- You will be inheriting property, money, or investments that will make up 50 per cent or more of your retirement savings.
- You have no company pension or partner with a pension, but you do have a good stable income and a long time frame (twenty years or more).

3: Moderately conservative

- You have a defined contribution pension plan, group RRSP or defined benefit pension plan that is likely to provide between 25 and 50 per cent of your retirement income needs.
- You don't mind taking a few financial chances but not too many.
- You are likely to have some debt in retirement.
- You are an older parent.

4: Fairly conservative

- You are young (under thirty-five) with a very long time frame (thirty to forty-five years) and understand that you don't need to take an aggressive investing approach

because the effect of compounding and long growth will
produce a strong return over time.

- You have a disability or family health concerns, or expect
  to have such concerns in the future.
- You are recently divorced or separated and/or suffered a
  financial setback.
- You experienced significant losses in the three recent
  stock market meltdowns.

5: Very conservative

- You won't have a company pension plan, or if you do have
  one, it will be very small.
- You are a contract worker or someone with little job
  security.
- You are over fifty and recently separated or divorced.
- You have less than ten years left to save for your
  retirement.
- You are young and willing to sacrifice the possibility of
  some growth for the safety and security of your money.
- You'd rather not worry too much about what is going on
  in the stock market.
- You are in the middle years and may have only ten to
  fifteen years of contributing to a company pension.
- You don't like financial risk—the thought of losing money
  makes your stomach churn!

These are all factors to take into consideration when selecting
your asset allocation. As you can see, a young investor might be
just as well suited to the most conservative approach as an older
person on the verge of retirement or someone who is very risk
averse. Conversely, a sixty-five-year-old with a civil service pension and no debt (like my dad) could choose the least conservative
strategy, even if another person in a similar situation but with a
different temperament might choose to take no risk whatsoever.

Pick Your Asset Allocation (AA)

The aim here is to make things simple and to keep fees as low as possible, while taking into account who you are as an investor. In this section, I'm going to introduce you to a few individuals and couples in various life stages and show you the asset allocation they have chosen.

You'll see that these real-life examples don't precisely match up with the scenarios outlined above. Don't worry if you don't fit exactly into one of these AA profiles either. Whether you have 50 per cent in equities or 60 per cent is less important than choosing an allocation in the first place and then doing the occasional housework to rebalance and maintain it.

> If you are uncertain what your asset allocation should be, always choose the more conservative profile. It is easy to add risk but can be very painful to get rid of it, especially after a market meltdown.

These sample allocations are deliberately quite broad. I am not cluttering them up with lots of investment options. If you're interested in emerging markets or precious metals or micro-caps (very small companies), you can always add them in later. For a knowledgeable investor willing to do more work or one using the services of an astute adviser, these asset allocations can be the core of a portfolio to which additional investment components are added.

Over time, simple asset allocations with a small number of investments (like the Easy Chair) will suit most investors and most situations, and will generate as good or better a return than more complicated portfolios.

After you choose your asset allocation you can move on to the next phase of actually picking the investments.

Case Study: Savannah, 26

Category 1: Least conservative
- single, renter
- no kids
- marketing account manager, income $42,000
- group RRSP contributions of $200 a month
- self-directed RRSP contributions of $200 a month

Self-directed RRSPs are what you open at a discount or full-service broker. They differ from workplace pensions because you (with or without an adviser) have control over the investments in the account.

Savannah has been on the job for a year after graduating with a degree in marketing and journalism. Her employer is matching 50 per cent of her group RRSP contributions up to $2,000 annually. Savannah is contributing enough to get the maximum from her employer but she also wants to save outside the company plan. Her industry is very mobile and chances are she will have a number of different jobs over the years, so she wants to have a self-directed RRSP that is under her control.

Savannah is young, with no dependents and no debts. She has chosen a more aggressive allocation because she feels very confident about her ability to earn at a higher level in the future, and she also wants the most growth possible in case she has an interruption in her earnings while raising a family. When she signed up with the company's group RRSP, she ticked the box marked "highest risk" when she selected her investment package. There were no ETF options presented to her (which is typical), only mutual funds.

I did warn her that a more aggressive mix might not necessarily produce the highest return, but she has decided to swing for the fences anyway and will re-evaluate in five years or so.

Savannah's asset allocation

Bonds:	20 per cent ($40 monthly)
Canadian equity:	50 per cent ($100 monthly)
US equity:	30 per cent ($60 monthly)

You'll note that Savannah has no cash in her RRSP. She is also saving $100 a month, in a TFSA, for the down payment on a condo; her parents are matching those contributions. In the future she is planning to deposit her tax refund into her TFSA. She could get a bigger tax break if she contributed that money to an RRSP and planned to draw it out through the Home Buyers' Plan, but she doesn't like the idea of paying the money back post-purchase.

Case Study: Kathleen, 59

Category 2: Mildly conservative
- recently divorced, small mortgage
- two adult children
- self-employed accountant, income $72,000
- RRSP contributions of $750 a month

Kathleen has $145,000 in a group RRSP from a previous employer (now transferred to a LIRA) and $130,000 in an RRSP, but she hasn't saved as much as she would like. Before her divorce, she had been counting on her husband's civil service pension. She intended to retire at sixty but now plans on working full-time until sixty-five. She is going to leave her LIRA alone for the time being and focus on her RRSP.

Kathleen is willing to take a few risks with her portfolio because she doesn't expect to need the money until she converts to a RRIF, which gives her a time frame of twelve years. You'll note there is no cash investment here. Kathleen has already set aside $15,000 in her TFSA for emergencies. She has all the money invested in GICs, so she is comfortable with this no-cash mix.

Kathleen's asset allocation

Bonds:	25 per cent ($187.50 monthly)
Canadian equity:	40 per cent ($300 monthly)
US equity:	20 per cent ($150 monthly)
International equity:	15 per cent ($112.50 monthly)

As an accountant, Kathleen knows money but she is not confident about investing, which is why her current RRSP is full of poor-quality, high-fee mutual funds. Some of her funds have deferred sales charges (DSC), so it may be wiser withdrawing the allowable 10 per cent annually than selling them completely. However, two funds (a health sector and a global fund) are such wretched performers that even if she takes a bit of a hit on the DSC fee, she will be better off in the long run. She does have one excellent mutual fund (an international fund) and was considering keeping it. I've told her this may make it more difficult to maintain her asset allocation if she is dealing with a combination of ETFs and a single fund. We compared her international fund, which has been in the top 25 per cent of similar funds, to one of the international ETFs I listed in chapter 14. The international fund *has* outperformed that ETF—which is rare—but not dramatically. So Kathleen has elected to go with simplicity and transfer her entire RRSP to the passive approach.

Case Study: Rosa, 53, and Salvatore, 57

Category 3: Moderately conservative
- four children, two still in university
- Rosa, assistant grocery store manager, income $38,000
- Salvatore, loans officer with a credit union, income $64,000
- Self-directed RRSP contributions of $200 a month for Rosa and $300 a month for Salvatore (into a spousal RRSP), plus both have defined contribution workplace pensions

Spousal RRSPs can be opened by one spouse in the name of the lower-earning partner. The contributor still gets the tax deduction. Spousal RRSPs are helpful to lower the taxes of the contributor and even out post-retirement income, thus reducing the tax bill and potential government clawback.

Rosa has spent five years contributing to her employer's group RRSP, and Salvatore has been contributing to his for nineteen years. They are hoping to retire when Salvatore is sixty-two and earn a small post-retirement income from growing spring flowers on their three-acre property. They have also been contributing to self-directed RRSPs ever since they stopped making RESP contributions for their kids. Rosa's RRSP has $26,000 and the spousal stands at $39,000. Both are invested in a variety of mutual funds. Half of them have not performed well in the last few years, about a quarter are moderately good, and a handful are top performers. The biggest problem with their RRSP portfolios, when

I took a look, was that they had a tremendous amount of duplication, with multiple funds investing in similar areas.

Rosa and Salvatore's new asset allocation

Cash:	10 per cent ($20 Rosa, $30 Salvatore)
Bonds:	30 per cent ($60 Rosa, $90 Salvatore)
Canadian equity:	40 per cent ($80 Rosa, $120 Salvatore)
US equity:	20 per cent ($40 Rosa, $60 Salvatore)

They have chosen a slightly more aggressive mix than the age rule, with 60 per cent in equities, because both of them can easily work part-time past age sixty if they need extra money. Once they near retirement they intend to chop their equity to 50 per cent, and then they'll cut it again to about 25 per cent by age sixty-eight or seventy.

Case Study: Marichka, 41

Category 4: Fairly conservative
- divorced, condo owner, $90,000 mortgage
- one child
- freelance set dresser for TV, theatre, and film, income averages $40,000
- savings of $300 a month

Marichka has been putting all her RRSP contributions into one-year GICs because she didn't know what else to do. She didn't lose any money during the market tumbles of the past decade, but now she wants the opportunity for a little more growth. She also wants a portfolio she can understand.

Marichka's asset allocation

Cash:	33 per cent ($100 monthly into TFSA)
Bonds:	33 per cent ($100 monthly into RRSP)
Canadian equity:	33 per cent ($100 monthly into RRSP)

Marichka can easily manage this allocation without too much work or fuss. She has $28,000 in her current RRSP, which she is going to split evenly between bonds and Canadian equity as soon as her GIC comes due. She will deposit $100 monthly into each of the bond and Canadian equity portions of her RRSP. Another $100 a month will be deposited into a TFSA; I suggested she do this because she has a freelance income and currently very little savings outside her RRSP. Her TFSA will serve as an emergency fund. As it grows with her contributions and interest income, she can always transfer some of it into her RRSP.

Marichka is unwilling to invest in the United States because she has friends and relatives there who have suffered deeply from the housing crisis and earlier financial scandals such as Enron. One cousin lost a good chunk of her pension funds in that accounting debacle.

You might consider this a very conservative allocation for someone of her age with a small amount of savings. Perhaps it would be better for her to choose a more aggressive portfolio and try to build up her RRSP. That certainly would make sense if we absolutely knew that equities would provide the most growth over the next twenty years. It could well be the case, but I don't know, just as I didn't know that equities would produce such low returns over the past ten years on an average annual basis.

Furthermore, Marichka has never invested in anything but GICs. For her, putting one-third of her savings into the Canadian stock market is a big leap.

Case Study: Gohind, 42, and Dawn, 41

Category 5: Very conservative
- recently married
- no kids
- career military officers, household income $156,000
- RRSP contributions of $400 a month each

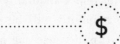

Gohind and Dawn are a military couple (midrank officers) who will have guaranteed government pensions. However, they are both ultraconservative financially.

Because Gohind and Dawn have spent their working lives in military housing in Canada and around the world, neither has ever owned a home. On retirement in ten years (at age fifty-two), they hope to buy a small farm on Vancouver Island and are planning to use one pension to make mortgage payments and cover housing costs and the other for living expenses and savings. The area is getting quite expensive and probably will be in the future, so they are prepared to have a mortgage into their seventies.

In addition, Gohind intends to bring his mother and one aunt from India to live with them. Neither woman has any assets, though they each have a small income that covers personal needs. They come from a family of very long-lived women. Both grandmothers and four of five great-aunts are over ninety. The women will rent an apartment together near Esquimalt, where Gohind and Dawn are stationed. On retirement, the mother and aunt will live with Gohind and Dawn in whatever property they end up purchasing.

Taking into account all these factors, Gohind and Dawn don't want to take any risks with their RRSPs, especially since they may be withdrawing funds from them through the first-time Home Buyers' Plan to help with their down payment. They both have TFSAs with $20,000 each, and they intend to maximize their contributions every year until they retire.

Gohind and Dawn's asset allocation
Bonds:	80 per cent ($320 each)
Canadian equity:	10 per cent ($40 each)
US equity:	10 per cent ($40 each)

Since Gohind and Dawn are also contributing $5,000 annually to their TFSA and investing that money in one-year GICs, they have left cash out of their RRSP asset allocation.

In Summary

These asset allocations show you how situation and temperament dictate how you invest. Don't worry too much about the exact percentages. The maintenance of your allocation through rebalancing and reinvesting income is the most important thing over time. Also, though I have used percentages to make for easier reading and to match what I have discussed in previous chapters, you can choose an even dollar figure for simplicity.

For example, Kathleen has arranged an automatic transfer of $750 every month from her chequing account into her RRSP. She has chosen to invest 25 per cent in bonds, which amounts to $187.50. If she invests monthly she can always round the amount up to $190. Though Kathleen is not going to have cash as part of her RRSP, she will inevitably have a small amount of cash in the portfolio at all times as dividends and interest income accumulate. She will eventually reinvest that money according to her asset allocation, but she can also use it to top up an investment amount if she needs a few extra dollars.

Again, don't get hung up on being exact, in terms of either the dollar figure or the percentage. The key is to stick close to your asset allocation over time, while keeping the overall process and the investments simple and comprehensible. And remember to always opt for a more conservative asset allocation if you are in the slightest doubt about your decision.

The next chapter lays out some sample portfolios, but it also shows you the mechanics of investing your chosen asset allocation in either ETFs or index mutual funds.

CHAPTER 17

Count On Yourself Portfolios

Buckle your seat belts! Here we go!

In the previous chapter, we looked at a variety of asset allocations. Remember that these allocations aren't hard and fast. There is no right or wrong. As long as you diversify among your three investment baskets—cash, fixed income, and equities—you will be fine.

When I was planning this section of the book, I intended to include three or four chapters full of sample portfolios. The women in the focus group said that's what they wanted. After all, who would buy a cookbook with only a couple of recipes in it? But eventually I realized that I would be giving in to the very thing that fells most investors, drives down returns, spreads confusion, and increases profits for investment companies—complexity. You don't need it.

With the passive method, it's not a particular portfolio that's important—it's the combination of asset allocation, ultra low fees, and rebalancing. So instead of offering numerous different options, I am simply going to lay out two modern versions of the original Easy Chair from chapter 12, one using ETFs and the other using index mutual funds. You can alter these two basic portfolios to fit your situation by changing the mix with more equities, less cash, etc. The beauty of both versions of this tried-and-true portfolio is their simplicity. Whether you choose the same asset allocation or vary it, you are dealing with only four investments.

However, because I recognize that some people feel compelled to buy stuff—even stuff they don't need—I will outline in the final chapter a couple of additional variations on the original Easy Chair for those who want more income and those who hope to achieve higher rewards by taking on more risk.

Portfolio 1: The ETF Easy Chair

Step 1: Who Are You?

- Moderately to fairly conservative (from the risk categories in chapter 16)
- Any age
- Investing in an RRSP, RESP, RDSP, RRIF, or non-registered account
- Medium to very long time frame (ten to over thirty years)
- Have $50,000 or more in your RRSP *and/or* are investing $500 or more monthly
- Investing a lump sum (inheritance, windfall, legal settlement, workplace buyout) *and/or* selling your current investments and switching to index investing

Note: The exceptions to the above conditions are those with Scotia iTrade accounts or who choose an all-Claymore ETF portfolio (more on this later). Scotia iTrade has recently abolished trading fees on nearly fifty ETFs, so you can buy fee free with small amounts monthly. Claymore also offers smaller investors an automatic investment plan for its ETFs and very low minimum monthly purchases. As this book goes to press, there are many changes in the ETF universe, and other providers or brokerages may offer similar programs for those with small amounts to invest in ETFs monthly.

Step 2: Asset Allocation

When the original Easy Chair was created in 1997, foreign content rules didn't allow you to invest more than 15 per cent of your RRSP funds outside Canada. Everybody kicked about it back then. But that restriction has actually proven to be very sound. Today, you can increase the US portion if you wish, but I wouldn't make it any more than 25 to 30 per cent of your overall portfolio.

The Original Easy Chair
- 20 per cent cash
- 30 per cent bonds
- 35 per cent Canadian equity
- 15 per cent US equity

Step 3: The Investments

ASSET CLASS (PER CENT)	ETF (PICK ONE IN EACH CATEGORY)	MER (PER CENT)
Cash (20)	GIC (no more than one-year term)	0
Fixed Income (30)	**XCB**—iShares DEX All Corporate Bond Index***** *or*	0.42
	XSB—DEX Short Term Bond Index***** *or*	0.26
	ZAG—BMO Aggregate Bond Index *or*	0.28
	CBO—Claymore 1–5 Year Laddered Corporate Bond ETF	0.27
Canadian Equity (35)	**CRQ**—Claymore Canadian Fundamental Index****** *or*	0.72
	XIC—iShares S&P/TSX Capped Composite Index**** *or*	0.25
	ZCN—BMO Dow Jones Canada Titans 60 Index *or*	0.15
	XIU—iShares S&P/TSX 60 Index***	0.15
US Equity (15)	**XSP**—iShares S&P 500 Index*** *or*	0.25
	ZUE—BMO US Equity Index*** *or*	0.22
	CLU—Claymore US Fundamental Index***	0.72

You'll note that I have included star ratings with some of my suggestions for your own Easy Chair–style portfolio. These were created by morningstar.ca and are performance-based. In other words, the closer an ETF sticks to the index it tracks (after fees), the higher the rating it gets. A fund must have more than three years of history to get rated, which is why newer funds are not yet rated.

I have given you four choices in the fixed income asset class. I've chosen corporate or corporate/government mix ETFs to give you a higher yield, roughly 1 to 1.5 per cent more at the time of writing. Any of this group will perform well for you.

For Canadian equity, there are also four choices. The first two track broader indices with more companies, and the last two track the S&P/TSX 60 Index with fewer and larger companies. All four have a dividend yield that is similar, but over time the ETFs tracking the S&P/TSX 60 Index should have a higher yield because that index includes big dividend payers such as the banks. If you close your eyes and pick with your finger, you will do fine with any of them.

And finally, I have listed three US equity ETFs. In chapter 14, I showed more choices in this category, but I like the ones here best because they represent a broader group (the S&P 500 Index) and will give you exposure to most sectors, including companies such as Apple.

Step 4: How to Do It

Follow these eight simple steps:

1. If you don't already have one, open a discount brokerage RRSP account through your bank or at one of the other discount brokerages such as Qtrade, Credential Direct, or Questrade.
2. Set up an automatic monthly transfer into your RRSP from your chequing or savings account.

3. Invest semi-annually if you're contributing $500 a month and quarterly if your monthly contributions are $750 or more (to keep trading costs low). Let the monthly deposits sit in cash until you are ready to invest.

4. Make your bond and equity ETF purchases first (see below).

5. To determine how many units you can purchase, type the ticker symbol into the Quote window on your brokerage's home page for the current trading price.

6. Divide the dollar amount you are investing by the trading price to get the number of units you can buy. Round up or down.

7. Make your GIC purchase with whatever is left over.

8. Go about your business knowing that you have put in place a great little low-fee portfolio that will beat most mutual funds and stock portfolios hands down.

Cost to invest: $29.85 every six months (with $9.95 trading commissions), or $59.70 annually. The trading costs will be higher if you invest quarterly or monthly and lower if you qualify for $6.95 trading commissions.

Note that because you purchase ETFs as you would stocks, you can't buy fractions of a unit at most brokerages. Make your bond and equity ETF purchases first, then put whatever is left, after the trading fee, into a GIC (or simply leave it in cash until there is enough to buy a GIC).

Because the cost per unit of the bonds and equity ETFs changes over time depending on the market, the number of units you're able to purchase will vary. The percentages for your asset allocation won't be exact, but that doesn't matter over time.

Lifeline for the math challenged! Don't feel bad if you have trouble working out percentages. Skills like that can get rusty in a very short time. Here's what to do if you have trouble: call up your brokerage (or go into your bank and ask to speak to one of the investment advisers) and tell them how much you have to invest and what your breakdown (asset allocation) is, and they'll tell you how many units you should buy. You can actually do this on the phone with your brokerage firm, and as long as you input the trade yourself, you won't pay a premium fee for what is called a broker–assisted trade.

Case Study: Sheleigh, 43

Sheleigh is divorced with no children and has a small mortgage on her condo. She owns a dog-grooming business with one employee. For the past twenty years, she has been making regular RRSP contributions, and her portfolio is now worth $88,000. She qualifies for low-cost trading fees of $9.95 at her bank.

Sheleigh has sold all the mutual funds in her existing RRSP. Her current RRSP contributions are $500 a month. She created her new passive portfolio according to the original Easy Chair allocations. It looks like this:

Cash:	one-year GIC	20% or $17,600
Fixed income:	bond ETF	30% or $26,400
Equities:	Canadian ETF	35%, or $30,800
Equities:	US ETF	15%, or $13,200

Twice a year, Sheleigh sits down at her computer, signs on to her brokerage account, and invests the $3,000 from her monthly contributions, as well as whatever interest income and dividend payments have accumulated. There is a little bit of math involved, but since the percentages for each investment remain the same (unless she changes her asset allocation or amount of contribution), she only needs to calculate how many units of each ETF she can buy that day. That will, of course, change each time depending on the markets and interest rates.

Sheleigh makes her three ETF investments first, and whatever is left over stays as cash in the account. Once a year (because her brokerage, like many, offers only one-year GICs), she will roll over her GIC, adding to it the roughly $1,200 that will have accumulated from her monthly contributions.

There will be a bit of cash remaining in the account, even after she rolls over her GIC. She doesn't need to worry about that, as the cash can help her round up or down future ETF purchases. This is how one investment session looked in mid-2011:

ASSET CLASS (PER CENT)	INVESTMENT	AMOUNT AVAILABLE	COST/ UNIT	UNITS PURCHASED	COST INCLUDING FEE
Cash (20)	GIC (eventually)	$ 600			$ 579.30
Bonds (30)	XSB	$ 900	$28.70	31	$ 899.65
Canadian Equity (35)	XIC	$1,050	$22	48	$1,065.95
US Equity (15)	XSP	$ 450	$15.35	29	$ 455.10

Sheleigh goes through this exercise every six months. The first couple of times it took her an hour or so. Now it takes less than thirty minutes. Remember I asked at the beginning of the book if you thought you could spare thirty minutes a month to take care of your investing life? It only takes Sheleigh thirty minutes twice a year!

$

I've used all iShare funds in this example for simplicity. Refer to the list in chapter 14 for other ETFs in the bond, Canadian equity, and US equity categories. Any of the ones listed in those tables will be a good choice. If she chose an all-Claymore lineup, she would set up a fixed monthly investment instead. If she had a Scotia iTrade account, she could do the same with a mix of ETFs and no fees.

Sheleigh's only other housekeeping chore is checking her asset allocation periodically, usually at the six-month point when she invests her $3,000. Her statement is divided into those three categories, or baskets—cash, fixed income, and equities—with percentages next to each one. If any have strayed too far from her chosen allocation—I use 5 per cent as my yardstick—she will use her new money to buy more of whatever is on the low end to regain the balance in her portfolio.

For example, if Sheleigh's Canadian equity portion (the XIC units) jumps from 35 to 42 per cent because there's been a big run-up in the Canadian stock market, she can use new contributions, plus accumulated interest and dividends, to buy more of the other three portions (cash, bonds, and US equity) to bring the percentages back to the original allocation. This isn't a complicated or time-consuming task.

Still, rebalancing can be challenging for many investors at first. "Why sell a winner?" is a refrain I've heard so often. The reason to sell is that winners rarely remain winners forever. By pruning back to your original allocations, you are doing what the big girls and boys on Bay and Wall streets do: taking profits and then putting them into something that is temporarily at a low ebb. When you rebalance, you don't need to ask yourself difficult and unanswerable questions, such as "Is the US stock market going to recover?" "Is the gold and oil bull market over?" Instead, you simply look at your percentages and say, "Aha, Canadian equity is soaring and bonds are sagging. Time for an adjustment." The asset allocation is your discipline.

And remember, if you are adding new money, most of the time you don't even need to sell anything. After a big market run-up, you might simply invest your new money in cash and bonds and wait to see where the equity percentage is the next time.

The other challenge for DIY investors is, again, the math. Damn those numbers! Don't fret about being exact. Just eyeballing your statement will likely tell you if any of your asset classes are straying to far from your original percentages. In most cases, you'll see the most change in two categories, the Canadian and US equities.

ETF EASY CHAIR ALTERNATIVE 1

Canadian ShareOwner Investments (www.investments.shareowner .com) started life in 1987 as a co-op buying "club" that allowed investors to make small purchases of stocks on a regular basis—monthly, quarterly, or annually. It was a terrific option in those days of high trading fees for people who wanted to assemble a portfolio of stocks.

Today, ShareOwner has expanded to provide cheap buying options for those who want to put money in ETFs but don't have large amounts to invest monthly. For a low price of $9.95 per trade, you can buy a small quantity, even fractions, of a variety of ETFs. Once you set up a brokerage account with ShareOwner (just as you would a self-directed account at a bank brokerage), you decide how much you want to invest, how often, and in which ETFs. ShareOwner does the rest, even reinvesting your dividends for you. It couldn't be easier.

Most of the ETFs available for purchase with a ShareOwner account are in the iShare stable. The chart that follows contains only those Canadian-listed ETFs I have mentioned in this book. However, ShareOwner does allow you to buy many funds, including sector and country ETFs (e.g., energy, retail, agriculture, Brazil, Japan), as well as ETFs listed on US stock exchanges. I'm not including those in this book because I don't think you need them. There are annual account fees from $50 to $100 ($79 for an RRSP). ShareOwner is a great choice for small investors, but keep your trades to quarterly or semi-annually to reduce fees.

Here's a sample portfolio you can put together and invest in regularly through ShareOwner. Pick one fund in each asset class.

ASSET CLASS	ETF (PICK ONE IN EACH CATEGORY)
Bonds	**XBB**—iShares DEX Universe Bond Index Fund (longer-term bonds) *or* **XSB**—iShares DEX Short Term Bond Index Fund
Canadian Equity	**HXT**—Horizons S&P/TSX 60 ETF *or* **XIC**—iShares S&P/TSX Capped Composite Index Fund *or* **XIU**—iShares S&P/TSX 60 Index Fund
US Equity	**XSP**—iShares S&P 500 Index Fund *or* **XDV**—iShares Dow Jones Selected Dividend Index Fund
International Equity	**XIN**—iShares MSCI EAFE (Europe, Australia and the Far East) Index Fund

Super simple and about as hands off as it gets in the investing world. The percentages you pick—that is, your asset allocation (discussed in chapters 9 and 10)—are dependent on your situation and time frame.

ETF EASY CHAIR ALTERNATIVE 2

Claymore Investments, which has a whole series of funds based on different indices than those used by the rest of the Canadian ETF world, offers an easy way to be a passive investor with as little as $50 a month per ETF. There is a dividend reinvestment plan (DRIP) and an automatic investment program (PACC, for pre-authorized cash contribution plan). You can sign up for both at www.claymoreinvestments.ca. You will need one enrolment form for each ETF. (Don't be distressed if your broker responds with confusion when you say you want to invest with Claymore. I've found that most staff at discount brokerages and banks are not that familiar with ETFs generally—let alone a program like the one Claymore offers. There's nothing complicated about it, but if you run into trouble just phone Claymore and ask for assistance.)

As of fall 2011, Claymore is also the only ETF provider that offers a cash investment—the Claymore Premium Money Market

ETF (CMR)—which makes it a true one-stop shop. CMR operates like a money market fund, but it has a very small MER of 0.22 per cent, and at the time of writing, the yield was a respectable 1.92 per cent. Not only is this as good as or better than most GICs, but the ETF is much more flexible and you don't need a large minimum to invest.

Perhaps the best part about a setting up a pre-authorized contribution Claymore portfolio is that the money comes right out of your bank account and into your investment account (RRSP, RESP, or any other). Of course, you can only purchase Claymore ETFs through this program, and you can't purchase fractions of units. The plan rounds your purchase to the nearest unit; any leftover cash can be used for the next month's purchase.

Here's a sample portfolio you could put together:

ASSET CLASS	ETF
Cash	**CMR**—Claymore Premium Money Market ETF
Bonds	**CBO**—Claymore 1–5 Year Laddered Corporate Bond ETF
Canadian Equity	**CRQ**—Claymore Canadian Fundamental Index ETF
US Equity	**CLU**—Claymore US Fundamental ETF

Like the Canadian ShareOwner example, the Claymore portfolio is super simple and hands off. If you choose either of these two routes, you should take a look at your asset allocation once a year or so and rebalance back to your original percentages if necessary. That might mean selling some of one or more categories. If the percentages are fairly close, leave everything as is and take another look six months later. The only other time I'd suggest being more vigilant is in the event of some kind of catastrophe. In 2008 and 2009, when the market was sinking faster than a block of concrete in a pond, your equity portions would have plummeted and you would have sold some cash or bonds and bought more equities. This isn't about timing the market. This is just about following the percentages. The result would have been a lovely gain as the market recovered throughout 2010 and 2011.

ETF EASY CHAIR ALTERNATIVE 3

If you are using a bank discount brokerage and decide to go with short-term bonds only, instead of bonds and cash, just increase your bond percentage. Or now that TFSAs are available, the cash part of your investments could be held there. However, it is still handy to have some cash in your portfolio so you can round up a trade and purchase an even number of units.

ETF EASY CHAIR ALTERNATIVE 4

Investors who are just starting out may have a bit of trouble with their cash investment because most discount brokerages require a minimum amount to purchase a GIC—typically $5,000 (though some, like TD Waterhouse, have a $1,000 minimum). Money market funds exist, but the return these days, after fees, is almost zero. One solution is to choose Alternative 2 and collapse your cash (GIC) allotment into bonds. This works well for smaller investors, especially if those who are accumulating cash elsewhere, such as in a TFSA.

A second solution is to put your cash in the Claymore Premium Money Market ETF (CMR), instead of waiting for it to accumulate in order to buy a GIC.

Portfolio 2: The Index Mutual Fund Easy Chair

Step 1: Who Are You?

- Moderately to fairly conservative (from the risk categories in chapter 16)
- Any age
- Investing in an RRSP, RESP, RDSP, RRIF, or non-registered investment account
- Medium to very long time frame (ten to over thirty years)
- Less than $500 monthly to invest or interested in keeping your investments automatic, even if you have to pay extra in management fees
- Not confident doing the math for the regular investments

Step 2: Asset Allocation

The AA for this portfolio is identical to that of Portfolio 1, though as I said at the beginning of the chapter, you can adjust these to fit your situation and temperament. The only difference in this portfolio is that it uses the index mutual funds I described in chapter 15.

- 20 per cent cash
- 30 per cent bonds
- 35 per cent Canadian equity
- 15 per cent US equity

Step 3: The Investments

ASSET CLASS (PER CENT)	INDEX MUTUAL FUND (PICK ONE IN EACH CATEGORY)	MER (PER CENT)
Cash (20)	GIC *or*	0
	Claymore Premium Money Market ETF	0.22
Bonds (30)	TD Canadian Bond Index-e *or*	0.49
	TD Canadian Bond Index	0.81
Canadian Equity (35)	TD Canadian Index-e *or*	0.32
	RBC Canadian Index *or*	0.70
	TD Canadian Index	0.86
US Equity (15)	TD US Index-e *or*	0.50
	Altamira US Currency Neutral Index *or*	0.63
	RBC TD US Index *or*	0.70
	TD US Currency Neutral Index	0.86

Once again, I have given you more than one choice in each asset class. If your investment account is with TD Canada Trust, pick the TD e-funds for the index mutual funds version of the original Easy Chair. At publication time, they were the best deal going for index mutual funds. You can only buy this series through a TD brokerage, however.

The fees for the non-e version of the TD funds are higher, but because you need only a $100 initial investment (turn back to chapter 15 to see all the minimum/subsequent investments), these index products are still a good choice for clients of other brokerages who have small amounts to invest.

The RBC Canadian Index fund is cheaper than its non-e TD cousin, but it does require at least $1,000 for the initial purchase and a minimum of $100 for each purchase thereafter. The Altamira and RBC US funds are also good competitors to TD, but both require $1,000 up front. However, subsequent investments can be made for as little as $50 and $25, respectively.

If you're completely new to index investing, or are just starting to take control of this aspect of your life but have only small amounts to invest, the TD funds will serve you very well because you can start investing right away without having to save up for a larger minimum purchase.

However, do check with your brokerage first. You may be able to invest with amounts as small as $25 per fund if you sign up for an automatic investment plan. This is a great boon to those contributing $100 or less a month and will allow you to make small monthly purchases of index mutual funds.

Step 4: How to Do It

Follow these four simple steps:

1. If you don't already have one, open a discount brokerage RRSP account at your bank or at one of the other discount brokerages such as Qtrade, Credential Direct, or Questrade.
2. Set up an automatic monthly deposit into your RRSP from your bank account.
3. Set up an automatic monthly investment plan with your discount broker for your three investments (one for bonds, two for equities), according to your asset allocation. All the brokerages have information about how to set up an automatic investment plan, but some are clearer than others. Call your brokerage and get help, if necessary.
4. Forget about it until it is time to rebalance—usually once a year or so.

Cost to invest: 0 (though there may be a charge to sell units)

If you're a nervous or confused newbie, I recommend going to your bank in person and getting help opening your account. Be aware, however, that bank advisers tend to push higher-fee, actively managed mutual funds; just be firm and explain that you want to be a passive index investor and will be purchasing only index mutual funds.

Also, since most advisers will naturally recommend their own bank's products, you will probably have to also be firm on the product you've chosen. A CIBC representative, for instance, may push you in the direction of the bank's own index mutual funds. However, CIBC had nothing competitive in this area at the point I was writing this book. If you get stuck at any point, call the discount brokerage directly. In most cases, you will get good information about how to manage your account, although you won't get advice on specific products.

The beauty of the index mutual fund portfolio is that, except for the occasional rebalancing, there is no regular management involved once you have set up your automatic purchases. One final note: you may also have to sign up for a separate program to automatically reinvest dividends and interest income. Make sure you ask as you are setting up your purchases.

Either of the two versions of the original Easy Chair (one with ETFs and one with index mutual funds) will function perfectly for 90 per cent of the people who read this book, but you may want to adjust the percentages to fit your situation, time frame, and temperament. These portfolios will give you a respectable return over time, while protecting your hard-earned savings from devastating loss. Even if you are tempted to add components, I highly recommend that you get familiar with the basic portfolio first.

In the next chapter, I'll show you how to adjust the portfolio so it produces more income, which will be handy if you're nearing retirement or need or want cash flow for some other reasons. I will also show you how to take on more risk, if you feel you must.

CHAPTER 18

Variations on the Theme

As I said at the end of the previous chapter, the basic Easy Chair portfolio will be perfect for 90 per cent of the people who read this book. However, there are some who need their portfolios to generate more income. For instance, if you are nearing or are already in retirement, you may have to start withdrawing funds from your RRSP or non-registered investment account. Or you may have just converted to a RRIF and are required to withdraw funds. With today's low interest rates, even a higher-income portfolio might not quite give you all the cash you need, but a steady flow of income could mean you don't have to sell quite so much from equities and/or bonds to meet your withdrawal demands. (If you are setting up any portfolio for income withdrawal, make sure you have a couple of years' worth of withdrawals in short-term GICs.)

> An income-generating portfolio isn't just for those at or
> near retirement; it could be used to provide revenue for a
> disabled family member, to meet child support obligations,
> or to finance all or part of a sabbatical.

The following portfolio is a higher-income variation on the Easy Chair theme. It includes a few more ETF products, but it still follows a passive, low-fee strategy.

Portfolio 3: The Income Easy Chair with ETFs

Step 1: Who Are You?

- Least to most conservative
- Any age
- More interested in regular income (dividends and interest) than pure growth and capital gains
- Medium to very long time frame (ten to thirty plus years)
- Have a portfolio of $25,000 or more *and/or* investing $500 or more monthly *or* you are going to use Claymore ETFs for most of your asset classes, invest through Canadian ShareOwner Investments, or have a Scotia iTrade account (in which case you can invest smaller amounts of money regularly)

Step 2: Asset Allocation

The following is a basic asset allocation for a passive (or index) income portfolio. It would suit someone with a moderate tolerance for risk and a need for income. Even if you have a less conservative outlook, be careful about increasing the equities portion. Don't forget that REITs and preferred shares are equities.

- 10 per cent cash
- 45 per cent bonds
- 10 per cent Canadian preferred shares
- 20 per cent Canadian dividend equity
- 10 per cent US dividend equity
- 5 per cent Canadian REITs

Happily, there are some excellent ETFs available for those who want to add preferred shares and real estate investment trusts (REITs) to their portfolio. You might recall that REITs are the primary kind of income or investment trusts that were not forced to change back to regular corporations in 2011. They make higher payments than most other equities, but they are still equities. However, the ETF basket itself means you have less chance of loss than you would if you bought a single REIT or even a handful of them. If one REIT in the index (and therefore in the ETF) falls flat, it won't have much impact. Also, the low MERs mitigate the risk to a degree; the less you have to pay out in fees, the more income is yours to keep.

Preferred shares are a hybrid of bonds and equities. Like bonds, they are issued with a set face value, usually $25, $50, or $100 per share. And like bonds, they come with a set payment (in this case a dividend). However, unlike bonds, the most common preferred shares (called perpetual preferreds) have no maturity date and continue paying the dividend until you sell them. Generally, preferred shares trade in a fairly narrow range. However, as interest rates rise the share value may decline (because the yield isn't as competitive).

Preferred shares offer higher yields than bonds because you are taking on more risk. If you hold a bond to maturity (assuming the company or government is stable), you are guaranteed to receive its face value—whatever that is. But with preferred shares, there is a risk of loss if you sell when prices have sagged. Despite that, preferred shares do have a place in an income portfolio for those wanting a known return over time. Like all ETFs, the basket of preferred shares protects you from gambler's ruin should one or more individual firms go under, as Royal Trustco did all those years ago, taking a big chunk of our money with it.

The asset allocation given above is just a guideline. If you need more income because you are close to retirement or already require income for living expenses, you can increase the percentage of preferred shares (just remember that while preferred shares are more stable than common shares, they are still equities).

If preserving your capital is more important than income, you should tweak your asset allocation to reduce the equities and increase the cash and bonds.

Step 3: The Investments

There is really little choice when it comes to index mutual funds that focus on income. (There are lots of actively managed income-oriented mutual funds, but fees will be higher for those.) As a result, this portfolio uses ETFs for income.

This ETF income portfolio offers you choice in most categories. I've listed the Claymore funds first because the dividend reinvestment and pre-authorized contribution plans make this portfolio possible even if you have only $50 a month to invest in each of the five funds. The all-Claymore portfolio is also a good choice if you are making monthly withdrawals, because the company has a systematic withdrawal plan (SWP). Enrol on the website at www.claymoreinvestments.ca. Note that there is no REIT offered by Claymore at the time of writing, but you can easily add either of the REITs listed below to your portfolio. If you are using Scotia iTrade, many (not all) of the ETFs listed are available for fee-less buying.

If you have a lump sum to invest, especially if you won't be making any new contributions (if you have a RRIF, for example, or yours is a non-registered account intended to give you income), you can mix and match. As I have mentioned before, competition is bringing about change to the ETF industry. Recheck with the ETF provider websites or your brokerage in case there are new options for automatic purchases or withdrawals.

Here are your best ETF options for this income portfolio:

ASSET CLASS	ETF (PICK ONE IN EACH CATEGORY)	MER (PER CENT)	YIELD (PER CENT)
Cash	**CMR**—Claymore Premium Money Market ETF**** *or*	0.22	1.92
	GIC	0	1.85
Bonds	**CBO**—Claymore 1–5 Year Laddered Corporate Bond ETF**** *or*	0.27	5.14
	ZAG—BMO Aggregate Bond Index *or*	0.40	3.56
	XCB—iShares All Corporate Bond Index Fund*****	0.42	3.62
Equities: Preferred Shares	**CPD**—Claymore S&P/TSX Canadian Preferred Share Index Fund**** *or*	0.50	4.7
	PPS—PowerShares Canadian Preferred Share Index ETF	0.45	—
Equities: Canadian Dividend Equity	**CDZ**—Claymore S&P/TSX Canadian Dividend**** *or*	0.66	3.43
	XEI—iShares S&P/TSX Equity Income Index Fund	0.55	2.95
Equities: US Dividend Equity	**CLU**—Claymore US Fundamental Index ETF*** *or*	0.72	1.99
	ZDJ—BMO Dow Jones Industrial Average	0.23	2.58
Equities: REITs	**ZRE**—BMO Equal Weight REITs Index *or*	0.55	5.9
	XRE—iShares S&P/TSX Capped REIT Index****	0.58	5.45

The yields listed will be different by the time you read this book. An easy way to find out the current yield is to visit the websites of the providers. All of them have a product list or ETF overview tab. In most cases, the yield will on the first page of the particular fund you are researching. You can also check out my site, www.countonyourself.ca, for the links. (Note that the PowerShares fund was too new to report yield at the time of writing.)

Step 4: How to Do It

Follow these six simple steps:

1. If you don't already have one, open a discount brokerage RRSP or other investment account through your bank or another discount brokerage.
2. Set up an automatic monthly transfer from your chequing or savings account into your RRSP or other investment account. (Obviously you won't take this step if the portfolio is intended for a RRIF or if you are withdrawing income regularly from an RRSP or any other account.)
3. Invest semi-annually if you have between $500 and $750 a month to contribute, and quarterly if you have $750 or more to invest (or sign up for the Claymore or Canadian ShareOwner pre-authorized investment program).
4. To determine how many units you can buy, type the ticker symbol into the Quote window on your brokerage's home page for the current trading price.
5. Divide the dollar amount to be invested by the trading price to get the number of units you can buy. Round up or down.
6. Go about your business knowing that you have put in place a low-fee, passive income portfolio that will beat most income mutual funds and stock portfolios hands down.

Cost to invest: This will depend on how often you are investing.

This income portfolio requires five investments. If you are concerned about managing them—that is, making the regular purchases according to your asset allocation and rebalancing occasionally—eliminate an equity investment. Right now, I'd choose to go without the US investment. You can always add it in later.

If you are investing a lump sum for income withdrawals, then you will simply make your investments and draw the income. But even in this case, you should take a look at your asset allocation once a year or so, and if one of the classes is on a tear or has dropped dramatically, use some of the income to buy more of what has sagged or sell some of the surging ETF to rebalance.

As with the portfolios in the previous chapter, you can adjust the proportions to suit your situation. And all income portfolios should have sufficient cash for at least two years of withdrawals—three is better.

$

Case Study: Ethel, 70

Ethel's husband died last year, and she is unable to manage in the family home even though she has professional assistance and family nearby. She is still physically okay but her memory is a little hazy. Her retirement income was adequate to meet her needs while she was living at home, but she'll need roughly an additional $19,000 when she moves into assisted living accommodations. The proceeds from the sale of her home are slightly over $500,000.

Happily, the four children get along well. Together with their mother, they have settled on the following asset allocation:

10% cash	($50,000)	in case of emergency
40% bonds	($200,000)	for stability and income
30% preferred shares	($150,000)	for income
10% Canadian dividend equity	($50,000)	for income and some growth
10% REITs	($50,000)	for income and some growth

They have chosen to drop the US component to keep things simpler. Here's how Ethel's passive ETF income portfolio looks:

ASSET CLASS	ETF	MER (PER CENT)	YIELD (PER CENT)	ANNUAL INCOME
Cash	**GIC**	0	1.85	$ 925
Bonds	**XCB**—iShares All Corporate Bond Index	0.40	3.56	$ 7,120
Equities: Preferred Shares	**CPD**—Claymore S&P/ TSX Canadian Preferred Share Index	0.50	4.7	$ 7,050
Equities: Canadian Dividend Equity	**XDV**—iShares Dow Jones Canada Select Dividend Index	0.5	3.97	$ 1,985
Equities: REITs	**ZRE**—BMO Equal Weight REITs Index	0.55	5.9	$ 2,950
Total				**$20,030**

Ethel's income portfolio provides more than enough cash to pay for the higher costs at the assisted living residence. One of her daughters has taken charge of monitoring the portfolio and has set up automatic withdrawals. Once a year, the daughter will pay a fee-only financial planner to help her ensure that the allocation remains close to the original. This portfolio is not without risk, since 50 per cent of it is in equities, but more than half of that is in lower-risk preferred shares.

Over time, the payments of the Canadian equity dividend ETF will grow as companies in the index increase their dividends. And if interest rates rise, the bond yield will also increase as bonds in the index mature and are replaced by others with higher interest rates attached. The same will be true of the GIC. (Of course, if this was 2007 and interest rates were falling, the reverse would be true.) The family may want to change the allocation in favour of more bonds as interest rates rise, which will reduce the risk in the portfolio.

Ethel's investments demonstrate how easy it is today to construct a passive income portfolio with low-fee ETFs. Please note that these are the ETFs the family settled on after consultation with an adviser. As I explained earlier in this chapter, there are numerous options in most of the categories.

I always feel a bit guilty about the Income Easy Chair—not to mention a portfolio like Ethel's—because it has so many investments, and unless you go with an all-Claymore portfolio or invest through the Canadian ShareOwner, you have more to manage and monitor than I'd like. If it seems like too much work to you, there is a one-fund option for an income portfolio. Yes, one single fund can do the income job for you. All three of the main passive providers offer a single ETF that contains other ETFs. Here are some income portfolio alternatives:

ETF	MER (PER CENT)	YIELD (PER CENT)
ZMI—BMO Monthly Income ETF	0.55	5.43
XTR—iShares Dividend Monthly Income Fund	0.57	4.30
CBD—Claymore Balanced Income CorePortfolio ETF	0.71	3.42

Beauty! A single exchange-traded fund gives you a regular stream of income paid monthly. These funds also do the rebalancing for you. Talk about hands off! These are very convenient and cost-efficient ETFs for a RRIF or any other investment account where you know you are going to be withdrawing income regularly. If you have a trust account for a child with or without a disability, for example, this is an easy way to invest the funds and have the income transferred to a bank account.

These ETFs are also very transparent. All three are a mix of equities and bonds (roughly 50 per cent in each). You'll note that the BMO ETF has a higher yield, but you shouldn't choose by yield alone. ZMI includes a higher proportion of riskier bonds, while the Claymore ETF includes more government bonds. If you are going to go this route, make sure you choose the ETF that fits your situation and temperament best.

These ETFs are good choices for those wanting regular income, but I'd advise adding more bonds if you have a RRIF, especially if you have no other source of income. Fifty per cent in equities is likely too high for someone in his or her late seventies or eighties. You can increase the bond portion by adding in any one of the bond ETFs listed in the ETF income portfolio table earlier in the chapter.

Case Study: Farida, 57

Farida is recently divorced. In the settlement, she received a lump sum of $280,000. She has been working part-time for the past twelve years as a civilian in a community police station, earning $21,000 annually.

Farida has never handled any money except for the portion of her earnings she deposited in her own chequing account monthly. She needs about $32,000 a year for living expenses now. She has $160,000 in a spousal RRSP, but she doesn't want to draw upon it until she's seventy-one.

She has chosen the ZMI-BMO Monthly Income ETF. The dividends and interest income (from her settlement) will amount to slightly more than $15,000 a year. Although the interest income from her settlement will be taxed at her regular rate, the dividend income will be taxed at a lower rate.

Farida will use $11,000 for living expenses and save the rest in a TFSA for emergencies.

There is some risk with Farida's choice because the BMO Monthly Income ETF is invested 50 per cent in equities and the market could take a bath as it did in 2008 and 2009. However, Farida has a reasonable time frame and plans on working past age sixty-five. By sixty-five, when she starts receiving her CPP and OAS payments, she will have built up cash in her TFSA; she can use that money to supplement her income until she converts her RRSP to a RRIF at age seventy-one.

She still may need to supplement her income between sixty-five and seventy-one because she expects to reduce her work hours. Assuming that happens, in four years she should start selling a portion of her income fund every year and investing the proceeds in a short-term GIC. Since she only has a single fund, this won't require much work; she can do it herself or consult an adviser at her bank. With a bit of luck in the form of rising interest rates and increased dividends, she may be able to maintain the $15,000 income, even though she'll be reinvesting in lower-returning GICs.

Farida suffered enormous stress with the breakup of her marriage, and she panicked at the idea of managing such a large amount of money. This option is not only convenient and inexpensive but she can understand it—and that is a big load off her shoulders.

I believe that the two passive portfolios presented in the previous chapter and the income options in this chapter will serve most people brilliantly. However, I recognize that the financial industry has convinced us that more product, scattered all over the world or focused on specific sectors, is better. If you find yourself unable to break out of this mindset, you aren't alone.

Last year, I had a conversation with the very savvy head of a large not-for-profit consumer financial agency. When I told him that the basic Easy Chair outlined in chapter 17 outperformed a souped-up but also passive portfolio with more investments around the globe and in specialty sectors such as technology, he didn't believe me.

Then I put together the returns for an ETF portfolio like the Easy Chair and for a portfolio that included an emerging markets ETF and a technology ETF. The boring, and much less risky, Easy Chair slightly outperformed the more aggressive portfolio over three, five, ten, and twenty years. He was gobsmacked when I showed him the figures.

Having said all this, I know the siren call of the investment industry is hard to resist, so I am including two (still passive) portfolios that have additional exposure to technology and emerging market countries. The first, for those with more money to invest, uses ETFs, and the second uses index mutual funds.

Portfolio 4: The ETF Racing Chair

Step 1: Who Are You?

- Least to moderately conservative
- Any age
- Fairly long time frame (fifteen-plus years) *or* shorter time frame but you have other sources of income
- You qualify for lower-fee trading and contribute $500 or more monthly
- You have a portfolio of more than $25,000

Step 2: Asset Allocation

Like all the other portfolios, this one has an asset allocation that can be adjusted for time frame, situation, and temperament. You can add bonds for more security or equity for more growth. I haven't included cash because more aggressive investors tend to avoid this asset class. But if you choose this portfolio, don't forget to build up a cash reserve somewhere else, such as inside a TFSA. In tough times, cash is still king, queen, and court jester.

- 30 per cent bonds
- 30 per cent large cap Canadian equity
- 20 per cent US and international equity
- 10 per cent emerging markets
- 10 per cent technology

Step 3: The Investments

ASSET CLASS	ETF (PICK ONE IN EACH CATEGORY)	MER (PER CENT)
Bonds	**CBO**—Claymore 1–5 Year Laddered Corporate Bond Index Fund**** *or*	0.27
	ZAG—BMO Aggregate Bond Index Fund *or*	0.28
	XCB—iShares All Corporate Bond Index Fund*****	0.40
Canadian Equity	**CRQ**—Claymore Canadian Fundamental Index Fund***** *or*	0.65
	XIC—iShares S&P/TSX Capped Composite Index Fund****	0.26
US and International Equity	**XWD**—iShares MSCI World Index	0.45
Emerging Markets	**CWO**—Claymore Broad Emerging Markets ETF**** *or*	0.46
	XEM—iShares MSCI Emerging Markets Index****	0.79
	ZEM—BMO Emerging Markets Equity Index ETF***	0.54
Technology	**ZQQ**—BMO NASDAQ 100 Index ETF**** *or*	0.35
	QQC—PowerShares QQQ (NASDAQ 100)	0.32

Step 4: How to Do It

Follow these eight simple steps:

1. If you don't already have one, open a discount brokerage RRSP or other investment account through your bank or at one of the other discount brokerages.
2. Set up an automatic monthly deposit into your RRSP (or other investment account) from your chequing or savings account.
3. Invest semi-annually if contributing $500 to $750 a month, and every quarter if contributing over $750. As I mentioned before, some ETFs can be purchased fee free with Scotia iTrade.
4. Make your bond and equity ETF purchases.
5. To determine how many units you can buy, type the ticker symbol in to the Quote window on your brokerage's home page for the current trading price.
6. Divide the dollar amount you are investing by the trading price to get the number of units you can buy. Round up or down.
7. As cash accumulates from interest income and dividends, add that to the amount you are investing.
8. Go about your business knowing that you have put in place a great little low-fee portfolio that will beat most mutual funds and stock portfolios hands down.

ETF RACING CHAIR ALTERNATIVE 1

If you choose Claymore ETFs where available (bonds, Canadian equity, and emerging markets), you can make those purchases monthly by enrolling in the pre-authorized plan. You only need a minimum investment of $50 per ETF.

Here's how a more aggressive portfolio using mostly Claymore ETFs would look if you had $400 to contribute each month:

ASSET ALLOCATION (PER CENT)	ETF	MONTHLY CONTRIBUTION
Bonds (30)	CBO—Claymore 1–5 Year Laddered Corporate Bond Index Fund****	$120
Canadian Equity (30)	CRQ—Claymore Canadian Fundamental Index Fund*****	$120
US and International Equity (20)	XWD—iShares MSCI World Index Fund	$ 80
Emerging Markets (10)	CWO—Claymore Broad Emerging Markets ETF	$ 40
Technology (10)	ZQQ—BMO NASDAQ 100 Index ETF	$ 40

The three Claymore ETFs are automatically purchased for your account each month once you set up the pre-authorized plan. The other two—XWD (international) and ZQQ (technology)—can be purchased every three or four months. Just leave those amounts in cash until you're ready to invest. This approach assumes you have enough bank business ($50,000 to $100,000) to qualify for lower commissions of $6.95 to $9.95 per trade. If you don't, then invest in those two funds annually. It isn't perfect because more regular investing (called dollar cost averaging) will smooth out market bumps more effectively. But if you have a long time frame, don't worry about it. Your portfolio will grow, and you will eventually become eligible for lower commissions and can invest more often.

A similar option is available if you open a Canadian Share-Owner account. Here's an example of how this more aggressive portfolio could look:

ASSET ALLOCATION (PER CENT)	ETF	MONTHLY CONTRIBUTION
Bonds (30)	**XSB**—iShares DEX Short-Term Bond Index	$120
Canadian Equity (30)	**CRQ**—Claymore Canadian Fundamental Index Fund*****	$120
US Equity (20)	**XSP**— iShares S&P 500 Index Fund	$ 80
Emerging Markets (10)	**XIN**—iShares MSCI EAFE Index Fund	$ 40
Technology (10)	**ZQQ**—BMO NASDAQ 100 Index ETF	$ 40

Note that at the time of writing, there is no ETF available through iShares that combines US and international equity, so I have substituted an all-US ETF. Also, there is no pure emerging market ETF, so I am using one that covers Europe, Australia, and the Far East.

Portfolio 5: The Index Mutual Fund Racing Chair

Step 1: Who Are You?

- Least to moderately conservative
- Any age
- Investing in an RRSP, RDSP, or non-registered account
- Longish time frame (fifteen-plus years)
- Less than $500 monthly to invest *or* interested in keeping your investments automatic, even if you have to pay extra in management fees
- Not confident doing the math for the regular investments and the occasional rebalancing

Step 2: Asset Allocation

The only difference between this portfolio and the previous one is that there is no index mutual fund that covers the world *including* the United States. Also, there is no reasonably priced emerging markets index mutual fund. Here is an asset allocation for more aggressive index mutual fund investors:

- 30 per cent bonds
- 30 per cent large cap Canadian equity
- 20 per cent US equity
- 20 per cent international equity
- 10 per cent technology

Step 3: The Investments

ASSET CLASS	INDEX MUTUAL FUND (PICK ONE IN EACH CATEGORY)	MER (PER CENT)
Bonds	TD Canadian Bond Index-e* *or*	0.32
	TD Canadian Bond Index	0.86
Canadian Equity	TD Canadian Index-e *or*	0.32
	RBC Canadian Index *or*	0.70
	TD Canadian Index	0.86
US Equity	TD US Index-e *or*	0.50
	Altamira US Currency Neutral Index *or*	0.64
	RBC US Currency Neutral Index *or*	0.70
	TD US Index	0.86
International Equity	TD International Index-e *or*	0.52
	Altamira International Index *or*	0.64
	TD International Index	0.98
Technology	TD NASDAQ Index-e *or*	0.50
	TD NASDAQ Index	0.99

*Remember that the inexpensive e-versions of these index mutual funds can only be purchased if you have a TD investment account.

Step 4: How to Do It

Follow these four simple steps:

1. If you don't already have one, open a discount brokerage account at your bank or other brokerage.
2. Set up an automatic monthly deposit into your investment account from your bank account.
3. Set up an automatic monthly investment plan with your discount broker for your five investments (one for bonds, four for equities) according to your asset allocation. All the brokerages have information about how to set up an automatic investment plan, but some are clearer than others. Call your brokerage and get help, if necessary.
4. Forget about it until it's time to rebalance—usually annually.

Last Words

The portfolios outlined in these last two chapters will serve most investors, from the most risk averse to those willing to take chances. The asset allocations are guidelines only and can easily be adjusted. Don't fret about picking the perfect AA. The key is to spread your eggs according to an allocation that works for you, then rebalance back to those percentages once or twice a year. In some cases, you may go a couple of years without having to rebalance.

Above all, remember the six golden rules:

1. KISS: Keep it simple, smarty!
2. Don't put all your eggs in one basket!
3. Be passive: This approach beats active mutual fund or stock portfolio management for most investors.
4. Fry those fees: This you will do by choosing either ETFs or index mutual funds.

5. Do your portfolio housekeeping: This will make the difference between cat food and caviar.

6. Don't sweat the small stuff: Don't worry about exact amounts or percentages. With ETFs, you will be rounding up or down to purchase whole units. With index mutual funds, you will be purchasing dollar amounts. Precision is a lot less important than following the program.

And there you have it—a simple, low-fee approach to investing. I have set up the portfolios so you can invest on your own, but they are equally suitable to put in place through an adviser. Over time, any one of these portfolios is going to beat the returns of most mutual fund or stock portfolios with similar asset allocations—even those managed by professionals. Best of all, they are ideal for those who want to follow the Count On Yourself approach in order to understand where their hard-earned savings are going.

Count On Yourself. Take the passive investing path. Then sit back and relax, because you are in control.

CHAPTER 19

The Bottom Line

So you've bought the program. At least I hope you have. There's a lot to digest in this book, and it may take time to understand everything—that's okay. The beauty of the Count On Yourself strategy is that it doesn't have to be complicated. In fact, the simpler you keep your portfolio, the better off you'll be. As I've mentioned before, there's absolutely no evidence that a portfolio full of complex investments will perform better than a simple one. Quite the opposite is true, as it turns out.

Now, you might be curious about how the index portfolios in this book, including the Easy Chair, have actually delivered over time. I don't blame you. It's hard to resist looking at performance and wondering how much money you are going to make. In the following pages, I'm going to provide return figures for four broad-based portfolios similar to those I discussed in the previous section. One is the Easy Chair, which I have been tracking for years. The other three are hypothetical portfolios, created by Morningstar's Andex Charts using broad-based indices—exactly the types of portfolios I am recommending for most investors.

Andex Charts are just about the coolest thing going when it comes to money. The charts show the relationship between world events and stock prices, interest rates, the price of oil, inflation rates, and the value of the dollar. It makes for fascinating browsing. You can get copies of fold-out Andex Charts from your bank or financial institution. New ones are released every fall. Go to www.andexcharts.com for more information.

Before you read the performance figures, it bears repeating that past performance is no guarantee of future results. You only have to look back to the events of 2008 or the dot-com bubble to know the truth of that. Also, the returns assume a lump sum of money invested and left in place over time. Most people, of course, don't invest like that. Unless Uncle Harry drops dead and leaves you a bundle, chances are you contribute to your RRSP (or any other investment account) over time, monthly, annually, or whenever you have spare cash.

The returns also don't take into account trading fees. However, because these have dropped dramatically in the past few years, this is no longer as big an issue, especially for a passive portfolio, where you're not doing a lot of buying and selling. Of course, if you invest with index mutual funds, you won't be paying a fee to buy (although there may be a fee to sell units when you rebalance). And if you enrol in either the Claymore or the Canadian ShareOwner systematic investment program, your investing costs will also be low. Also Scotia iTrade customers have nearly fifty ETFs for purchase with no fees.

The returns do assume that all interest income and dividends have been reinvested, and that the portfolios are rebalanced periodically to maintain the original percentages.

Finally, I have used pure index returns for the portfolios here, rather than the returns of specific ETF and index mutual fund products. Since I have offered you choice in most categories, these index returns will tell you how a similar portfolio, with ETFs or index mutual funds, would have performed over time. Your experience will differ, of course, and will depend on how you invest (lump sum, annually, etc.) and which products you choose. But I have recommended ETFs and index mutual funds, which closely track their index, so if you duplicate any of these portfolios with any of the index products mentioned, your return will be close to these hypothetical results. Once trading fees and MERs are taken into account, the actual returns will be somewhat different, but these figures will give you a window into what has gone on before.

In the following four portfolios, cash is a five-year GIC. The bond investment is a broad government and corporate index. Canadian equity is the S&P/TSX Composite Index. US equity is the S&P 500 Index. Global equity is the MSCI World Index (not including the United States). US small companies is the US Small Stock Total Return Index. To find this specfifc ETFs and index mutual funds that track these indices, go back to chapters 14 through 18.

1: Very conservative

Cash:	20 per cent
Bonds:	60 per cent
Canadian equity:	10 per cent
US equity:	10 per cent

2: Conservative (The Easy Chair)

Cash:	20 per cent
Bonds:	30 per cent
Canadian equity:	35 per cent
US equity:	15 per cent

3: Moderate

Cash:	10 per cent
Bonds:	30 per cent
Canadian equity:	20 per cent
US equity:	20 per cent
Global equity:	20 per cent

4: Aggressive

Cash:	5 per cent
Bonds:	15 per cent

Canadian equity: 25 per cent
US equity: 25 per cent
Global equity: 20 per cent
US small companies: 10 per cent

If you chose ETFs for any of the above portfolios, the figures below are close to the performance you would have experienced over time. You would have lower returns for index mutual funds because the fees are higher.

PORTFOLIO	1 YEAR (PER CENT)	3 YEARS (PER CENT)	5 YEARS (PER CENT)	10 YEARS (PER CENT)	20 YEARS (PER CENT)
1: Very conservative	8.1	5.2	5.5	6.3	8.7
2: Conservative	9.8	4.7	5.4	6.0	8.6
3: Moderate	13.4	2.7	3.9	4.7	8.4
4: Aggressive	16.9	2.2	3.0	4.0	8.8

Portfolios 1, 3, and 4 are based on hypothetical portfolios from Andex Charts as of June 2011.

Now, I can't let you go without encouraging you to cast your eye down the twenty-year column. The most conservative portfolio has performed as well as the more aggressive one. In fact, it has outperformed everything else, including the Easy Chair, in most time periods except the most recent. Of course, who knows what the future will bring? But these figures do emphasize the point that I've made throughout this book: higher risk doesn't necessarily translate into higher return, especially over time.

The path to Count On Yourself success is a simple portfolio, a handful of ETFs or index mutual funds, and a bit of housekeeping.

And that's it, folks. Go to my website, www.countonyourself .ca, for updates, templates, and other useful information.

Good luck! Count on yourself—you can do it!

RESOURCES

This list could extend to many more pages but these sites are among the best sources of information about ETFs, investing, and money management.

ETF Provider Websites

http://ca.ishares.com

www.etfs.bmo.com

www.claymoreinvestments.ca

www.horizonsetfs.com. Much of this site is devoted to the large stable of actively managed ETFs, but you will find information about the passive ones mentioned here.

www.powershares.ca

www.vanguardcanada.ca. This new entrant to the Canadian market announced its six new ETFs as this book was being written.

Other ETF Sites

www.cetfa.ca. The Canadian ETF Association was just forming as this book went to press.

www.canadiancouchpotato.com. This site is all about ETF investing, and you will find up-to-date information and industry news here. Dan Bortolotti does a thorough job.

Brokerages

In addition to bank brokerages you can also look at:

www.investments.shareowner.com

www.qtrade.ca

www.credentialdirect.com (owned by credit unions)

www.disnat.com (owned by Group Desjardins)

www.questrade.com

For a rundown of how the brokerages stack up, Rob Carrick provides an excellent broker ranking annually in *The Globe and Mail*, and it is highlighted on www.gold.globeinvestor.com.

General Investing Information

www.getsmarteraboutmoney.ca. This is an initiative of the Investor Education Fund, the educational arm of the Ontario Securities Commission. The site contains great tools and calculators, a good glossary, and lots of excellent content about money generally and investing specifically.

www.investopedia.com. I find this site very helpful for its in-depth glossary of financial and investing terms.

www.tmxmoney.com. The site of the Toronto Stock Exchange has a whole area devoted to ETFs.

www.morningstar.ca. This is one of my favorite sites for ETF information and solid articles.

For Families

www.bmo.com/smartstepsforparents. I admit a little bias here as I have worked with BMO to put together content for this site. That aside, it is very useful for parents who need answers about how to teach financial literacy to their children.

Debt and Credit

www.creditcanada.com. This wonderful not-for-profit charity has a ton of information about money as well as counseling. The website is very useful and so are the regular blogs.

Other Resources

www.moneysense.ca. *MoneySense* magazine does a great job of covering the ETF world specifically and investing generally.

www.canadianmoneysaver.ca. *Canadian MoneySaver* magazine also provides a wealth of very pragmatic financial articles.

www.theglobeandmail.com/globe-investor/personal-finance /personal-finance-reader. Rob Carrick's Reader: The best of the money blogs. Rob Carrick of *The Globe and Mail* compiles an eclectic list of money topics and blogs weekly (I don't think the man ever sleeps).

www.canadianbusiness.com. Despite the title, *Canadian Business* magazine has many consumer-friendly articles from excellent writers about all things personal finance and investing.

And, of Course, My Own!

www.alisongriffiths.ca

ABOUT THE AUTHOR

ALISON GRIFFITHS is an award-winning financial journalist, broadcaster, and bestselling author. She has hosted two acclaimed television shows—*Maxed Out* for W Network and *Dollars and Sense* for Viva—as well as *The Score*, a CBC sports magazine show; *Midday* (CBC TV); *Canadian Investor* (CTV); *The Inside Track* (CBC Radio); and *Morningside* (CBC Radio).

Alison writes the popular "Me and My Money" column for the *Toronto Star* and the "Alison on Money" column for *Metro*. Alison is the financial expert for BMO Smartsteps for Parents website, http://community.bmo.com/smartstepsforparents, and for Chicago-based BMO Harris Bank's Helpful Steps for Parents website, http://community.bmoharris.com/helpful-steps-for-parents. Thousands have turned out over the last few years for her seminar series on investing and money management; and she is also in demand as a speaker on money matters.

She has received awards from ACTRA (radio documentary), the Canadian Centre for Investigative Journalism, the Business Magazine Writing Award, the National Magazine Writing Award, the Canadian Railroad Historical Association (for *Lords of the Line*), and the Robert Wagner Screen Writing Award for the teleplay of *Net Worth* (produced by CBC).

With David Cruise, Alison Griffiths has co-written ten books. Their first work of fiction, *Vancouver* (2003), earned them a starred review in the U.S. based *Publishers Weekly*.

She and David Cruise divide their time between their two small farms in Ontario and Florida with their two dogs and three horses. They have two daughters and a grandson.